D0970350

Teaching Common Sense

Teaching Common Sense

The Grand Strategy Program at Yale University

Foreword by Henry Kissinger

Linda Kulman

WESTPORT AND NEW YORK

Published by Prospecta Press, an imprint of Easton Studio Press
P.O. Box 3131
Westport, CT 06880
(203) 571-0781
www.prospectapress.com

For Ralph, Sam, and Julia — my universe; and for JGK and ODK — who guide me, still. — LK

Designed by Barbara Aronica-Buck

First Edition
Manufactured in the United States of America
Hardcover ISBN: 978-1-63226-068-0
eBook ISBN: 978-1-63226-069-7

Contents

Foreword

Contemporary foreign affairs are generally being studied as anything but "grand," focusing on individual cases in a fragmented process that has challenged the capacities for comprehensive analysis.

The program in Grand Strategy at Yale University seeks to overcome this problem by conveying to future leaders — today's college, graduate, and professional students — both an intellectual understanding of and some operational experience in strategy and policy in a comprehensive structure for international relations. Regarding the importance of such analysis, I wrote long ago, "History is not a cookbook offering pretested recipes. It teaches by analogy, not by maxims. It can illuminate the consequence of actions in comparable situations, yet each generation must discover for itself what situations are in fact comparable. No academic discipline can take from our shoulders the burden of difficult choices." In the past decade and a half, I have observed and engaged with the faculty and students in the Grand Strategy program at regular intervals and have seen the seminar not only achieve the objectives of its founders by instructing students in history, strategy, and decision making, but also emerge as a model for educational emulation and a symbol for intellectual innovation elsewhere.

Today, in pursuit of "objectivity," the study of history is

shying away from policy recommendations, while schools of "policy studies," in pursuit of theoretical "rigor," are avoiding historical cases. This gap is what the Grand Strategy program knows it must learn to close. The program's challenge is to expand each generation's fund of experience without becoming overwhelmed. Thus, it begins with "the classics," distillations of experiences presented to be applicable to futures beyond imagination — an inherently evolving canon of works that from Sun Tzu to Thucydides to our own time has provided intellectual inspiration and shaped political institutions and practices. The greatest challenges to strategy and statecraft lie in the realm of unavoidable uncertainty, where decisions must be made before it is possible to know all the facts or to assess their ramifications. An education in the classics offers a leader a body of knowledge which can help prepare him or her for the necessity of taking action in moments of daunting uncertainty, including on matters critical to world order. In this sense, the Grand Strategy program has revived and reemployed a humanistic culture of learning and decision making that was once understood to be fundamental, yet in more recent times has largely been neglected.

I am proud to have been associated with this pioneering effort since its inception — with those who brought the idea into being: Paul Kennedy, John Lewis Gaddis, and Charlie Hill; those who have made the continued existence of the program possible: Charlie Johnson and Nick Brady; the two Yale presidents who have supported it: Richard Levin and Peter Salovey; and most recently, the new director of the Brady-Johnson Program in Grand Strategy, professor and master of Branford College Elizabeth Bradley. The efforts of these and other individuals are comprehensively described in this book. Not only has Linda Kulman chronicled the history of the program, she also has captured the learning that I have seen occur around the Grand Strategy seminar table when lively teachers, eager students, and great ideas converge. This book demonstrates how the program's approach, essential to our future, has both come into being and evolved.

Henry Kissinger
February, 2016

Preface

This history is based on reporting and research that I conducted intermittently over four years. From 2011 to 2015 I had an all-access pass to Grand Strategy seminars, crisis simulations, and class dinners, and the extraordinary cooperation of the professors and students, many of whom I spoke with more than once. I was also fortunate to interview Nicholas Brady, Charles Johnson, Henry Kissinger, Richard Levin, Peter Salovey, George Shultz, and Yale professors Scott Boorman, David Brooks, John Negroponte, Douglas Rae, Gaddis Smith, and Norma Thompson. Among the former program administrators with whom I spoke were Ted Bromund, Jeremy Friedman, and Caroline Lombardo.

Since the grand strategy of the Brady-Johnson Program in Grand Strategy is not to shape current policy but to train future decision makers, this history presents the results of a groundbreaking survey of 385 alumni enrolled in the class between 2000 and 2014, with the aim of seeing the program's long-term impact. Comments from former students make it clear that the professors achieved their goals, and I'd like to thank all of the participants for sharing their views.

I'm particularly grateful to the program's three founding professors, John Gaddis, Charlie Hill, and Paul Kennedy, for entrusting me with this project, to Elizabeth

Bradley for her inclusiveness and for enabling me to view Grand Strategy as a set of leadership principles, and to Sam Chauncey and Paul Solman for their insights and friendship. The help I received from Igor Biryukov, Kathleen Galo, and Elizabeth Vastakis was invaluable, with deepest thanks to Sara Rutkowski. Among former students, I'd like to single out Conor Crawford, Campbell Schnebly-Swanson, Justin Schuster, Isaac Wasserman, and Haibo Zhao, who were as generous as they are impressive. Chris Howell lent moral support to this project from day one, and later, his senior thesis on the intellectual history of grand strategy. Colonel Craig Wonson, the first Marine Corps fellow assigned to International Security Studies to provide a military perspective on grand strategy, graciously did the same for me.

Soon after I began reconstructing the program's history, I met with Paul Kennedy at Yorkside Pizza, a basic but venerable restaurant down the block from the university's Hall of Graduate Studies, where the Grand Strategy seminar usually meets. I popped open my laptop on the table between us as he began to describe what led the three professors to create the program. "Bring a tape recorder the next time we meet," Kennedy said. "While you're typing, you might miss a point I'm making."

As a journalist I had long ago concluded that taping interviews hindered rather than helped me in my reporting. I didn't pay as much attention to what was being said in the moment in the belief that I could go back and listen again. But too often the recorder malfunctioned, and even when it worked, I found most of what I didn't catch the first time of marginal value.

I did, however, tape my next conversation with Kennedy. Several months passed before I had an epiphany about why he'd insisted upon it. It happened one fall evening on the train from New Haven to Washington. Earlier that day Gaddis had moderated the Surprise and Intelligence class, a fall staple that focused on the decade-plus period between the fall of the Berlin Wall and 9/11, two unforeseen events that altered the world. The message had been to pay attention to everything. Kennedy, at Yorkside, had been giving me a subtle lesson on how the human mind works — actually a primer on Grand Strategy. He was telling me how difficult it is to process all of the information that comes at us.

When Nick Brady and Charlie Johnson, who endowed the Grand Strategy program and after whom it is now named, commissioned me to write this intellectual history in 2011, the question at the heart of my reporting was, how is critical thinking taught? The plan was for me to attend the Monday-afternoon seminar for a full year to capture the spontaneity, drama, and learning that occur in the GS classrooms and as many extracurricular presentations and dinners as practicable. I would also conduct interviews with the professors and current and former students. The final product, as Gaddis described it, was to be a narrative "rendered with a novelist's eye." I've used pseudonyms when I quote students in class unless permission was otherwise given, but the people are real and the other details about them have not been changed. If they agreed to be interviewed, I used their real names, except where specified, and quotations from these conversations and the classes that I attended are from my notes.

When I began this project the Arab Spring was a work in progress, Osama bin Laden was alive and hiding in a safe house in Pakistan, Muammar Gaddafi was the leader of Libya, the Crimean Peninsula was part of Ukraine, and the Islamic State of Iraq and the Levant (ISIL) had not yet become a horrifying household name. I was fortunate to witness each of these history-making changes through the lens of the class. I'm indebted to Nick and Charlie, above all, for my box seat and for their great generosity over the years.

Part One

What Is Grand Strategy at Yale?

Filling a Void

It's the first Saturday in December, three weeks before Christmas, and the president is having a hard day.[1] The Oval Office calendar was purposely light so the president could focus on a nationally televised policy address scheduled for 4:00 p.m. But by midmorning crises have jammed the mostly ceremonial agenda. Overnight, during a surge in protests by the Hong Kong pro-democracy Umbrella Movement, Chinese police took an American citizen with possible CIA or Taiwanese ties into custody at an undisclosed location. Also overnight the US Central Command confirmed that an American shoulder-launched AIM-92 Stinger missile downed an Iranian air force F-4 Phantom fighter-bomber conducting airstrikes against ISIL positions in Iraq, potentially jeopardizing the tenuous, unspoken non-aggression pact between the United States and Iran. Dire financial news coming out of Ukraine and Georgia has this morning's *Financial Times* insisting the United States take responsibility for the fall-out from sanctions against Russia "that it pushed so actively." Even an Oval Office grip-and-grin with the young athlete of the year threatens to backfire. The soccer star attends the University of Virginia (UVA), the setting for a recent *Rolling Stone* article recounting an alleged brutal gang rape of a female student by members of a local fraternity who, this week, disputed the allegations.

"I'm going to avoid any comment on sexual assault like the plague," the White House's new press spokesman, Arthur Knoop, says minutes before his first-ever daily briefing.

"Right," a presidential adviser agrees. "The way to dodge it is to say we're not going to comment on an ongoing investigation."

As Knoop walks in, the briefing room is crowded with members of the press corps, forty strong, seated in hastily arranged rows of stackable chairs. No one asks about UVA. But the reporters intend to hold the president accountable for other events, and Knoop, standing behind a podium at the front of the room, is scrambling to keep up.

"Can you tell us about North Dakota?" a journalist demands.

"North Dakota in what sense?" Knoop asks.

"There's been an oil spill in the capital," the reporter says, referring to news reports that a four-vehicle tanker convoy exploded south of Bismarck, halting traffic and spilling oil into the nearby Missouri River. "Congress is saying it's the president's fault."

"What's the president's policy on Keystone XL?" another reporter demands.

"Um . . ." Knoop hesitates.

"What about the hostage in China?"

"The president believes in free speech," Knoop answers.

"Why didn't the president bring this up in China?"

"When was the president in China?" Knoop asks.

"Last month."

"Aw crap."

Knoop's profanity quickly turns into a public relations

disaster for the White House. "Even this hardened, jaded, seen-everything media community was . . . shocked by . . . Administration Press Spokesman [Knoop's] expletive at this morning's press conference," a *Washington Post* editorial comments. "The question must be asked: is this the image [the president] wants to present to America's public?"

"Perhaps it's time for a Press Spokeswoman," tweets Foxes & Hedgehogs, a moderate political news outlet.

Calling for a congressional hearing, the Republican House majority leader tells conservative news agency Justice Now that Knoop's behavior "is just ineptitude, left and right, back and forth, diagonally."

Even German tabloid *Bild-Zeitung* joins in: "Oh Scheisse: 'Aw crap' crosses the Atlantic!" The newspaper continues: "Let the Americans pay for the c*** they deposited on our doorstep in Ukraine and Georgia. Why should Germany pay for the fallout from another act of aggressive American policy?"

The president's intentionally light calendar seems to be shredding.

But none of this is real.

It's part of an elaborate crisis simulation run by Yale University's Brady-Johnson Program in Grand Strategy. The Oval Office is a second-floor classroom in Linsly-Chittenden Hall (LC), a nineteenth-century Romanesque Revival brownstone, on High Street in New Haven, Connecticut. The president and vice president, both women, were elected by their classmates a couple of weeks earlier. Other students have been appointed to play cabinet secretaries, members of Congress, White House aides, or bloggers. What happens next depends on the professors and staff sitting around a scuffed oak table in the "control room" — another LC classroom — and a stack of handwritten cards laying out various fictional disasters.

Sometimes the note-card scenarios have closely paralleled subsequent actual events.

The two-day crisis simulation caps the Grand Strategy program's (GS) yearlong, admission-by-invitation, interdisciplinary course — a class in four acts that includes a spring semester spent mastering great books on statecraft and diplomacy; a summer experience that's supposed to be an "odyssey" in the Patrick Leigh Fermor tradition;[2] and a fall semester featuring military-inspired "murder boards," more delicately known as "Marshall Briefs" after soldier-statesman George C. Marshall's demand for brevity on some of contemporary society's most urgent issues. The year also includes a full schedule of extracurricular lectures, workshops, and off-the-record dinners with government officials, journalists, authors, poets, ambassadors, and other dignitaries — usually including former secretary of state Henry Kissinger.

GS was established in 2000 by Professors John Lewis Gaddis, Yale's Robert A. Lovett Professor of Military and Naval History and founding director of the program; Paul M. Kennedy, the university's J. Richardson Dilworth Professor of British History and founding director of Yale's International Security Studies Program (ISS); and Charles Hill, a "practitioner" professor who distinguished himself as a career Foreign Service officer before coming to Yale to teach full time. At a cost of $1.4 million annually,[3] the program is expensive. It's also an attention grabber. Two years before he joined its faculty as a practitioner professor in 2013, *New York Times* columnist David Brooks described the seminar as "the best course in America."[4] The class has been the subject of articles and blog posts in the *Wall Street Journal,* the *Nation,* and the *New Republic.* Most significantly GS attracted the notice of Nicholas F. Brady (Yale, '52) and Charles Johnson (Yale, '54), who endowed the program in 2006.

Brady, the longtime senior partner at a leading Wall Street investment banking firm, US senator, and treasury secretary under Presidents Ronald Reagan and George H. W. Bush, is best known for the Brady Plan, which resolved the 1980s international debt crisis. He went on to found Darby Overseas Investments, a pioneer in emerging markets private equity investment. Johnson is the retired chairman of Franklin Resources, a money management company that he led for nearly fifty years. One of the largest single-gift donors in Yale's history—for the construction of its two new colleges[5]—Johnson also underwrote renovations in Yale's athletic facilities and the Johnson Center for the Study of American Diplomacy, which supports research in the Kissinger papers at Yale. The two men believe that the Grand Strategy course fills a void in American higher education. "Colleges are turning out hothouse flowers," Brady said. "These overstudied, underexposed students need a course in common sense."[6] As he wrote in a monograph on common sense (defined as "sound, practical judgment in everyday matters") it's "a key ingredient in the best leadership."[7] "If you don't teach leadership and people aren't exposed to it," Johnson added, "they don't even know what they missed."[8]

Kissinger saw a similar gap. "I think one of the empty

spaces in our country . . . is the study of strategic issues," he commented. "We lack [the] preparation of a young leadership group . . . That is, how you assemble the issues that are relevant to national decision making and develop a habit of thought that you get to automatically. The American tendency is to wait for a problem to arise and then to overwhelm it with resources or with some pragmatic answers. But what you need is a framework of decisions that helps you understand where you're trying to go."[9]

Gaddis, Kennedy, and Hill, each of whom is now a Brady-Johnson Distinguished Fellow in Grand Strategy, built GS in response to Kissinger's observation that "the convictions that leaders have formed before reaching high office are the intellectual capital they will consume as long as they continue in office."[10] Unlike the performance-driven approach that's the subject of most motivational business books, their leadership model is character driven. "Education used to prepare people to think about the biggest and most complex questions of the human condition," Hill said. "That preparation was through literature and philosophy and classical texts, not through political science or psychology. You got psychology much better from great books than from the psychology professor who was working on a tiny corner of something."[11] The GS faculty anticipated, by more than a decade, higher education critic William Deresiewicz's complaint that what prestigious universities "mean by leadership is nothing more than getting to the top. Making partner at a major law firm or becoming a chief executive, climbing the greasy pole of whatever hierarchy you decide to attach yourself to. I don't think it occurs to the people in charge of elite colleges that the concept of leadership ought to have a higher meaning, or, really, any meaning."[12] Andrew Hacker and Claudia Dreifus in *Higher Education: How Colleges Are Wasting Our Money and Failing Our Kids—and What We Can Do About It*, echo the thought: "To our mind, *leadership* refers to a willingness and ability to rouse people to a party, a purpose, a cause," they write. "We're not convinced that what happens in classrooms or on campuses nurtures leaders more than other settings—than, for example, back roads of the Mississippi Delta or lettuce fields in California."[13]

A GS applicant's 4.0 grade point average, by itself, doesn't impress the professors. "We consider those people more drones than leaders," a former GS administrator said. Neither do enticements. One student application was personally delivered with an expensive box of chocolates, and another applicant's parents offered a "substantial" donation in exchange for their child's acceptance into the program.[14] Both efforts had the opposite effect. The selection committee aims to identify young people with eclectic backgrounds and a capacity for resilience[15] who will succeed at high levels—and provide them with tools to use when they get there. This is why the *Yale Herald* facetiously writes that GS is "also known as 'How to Rule the World: A Few Quick Tips.'"[16]

But the Brady-Johnson Program doesn't offer quick tips. Or quick anything. The course emphasizes students' ability to speak and think on their feet and to understand how parts relate to the whole. They are asked to consider how lessons of the past—successes and failures—may apply to the present and the future. Instead of handing out easy answers, GS inures students to uncertainty, based on the understanding that decisions, particularly in positions of responsibility, almost always have to be made before all of the facts can be gathered. We're trying "to equip young people to deal with the unforeseen," Gaddis said. "There's no way that we can predict what they'll be doing or what problems they'll be confronting."[17] And as Brady and Johnson recognized, common sense must be at the core of such preparation. It's "like oxygen," Gaddis remarked. "The higher you get the thinner it becomes."[18]

In its sixteenth year, the Grand Strategy Program is as recognizable to Yalies as the letter *Y* and the school's bulldog mascot, Handsome Dan. High school students often hear about the program even before they apply to Yale. Along with cultivating leadership skills the Brady-Johnson Program offers students a worldview. Many of the approximately five hundred women and men who have completed the program and are ascending the ladders of government, nonprofits, the US military, universities, and the corporate sector describe it as one of their most formative Yale classes — influencing them not just professionally, as might be expected, but also, personally. As Christopher Wells (GS '02) said: "For me, [GS] is a fundamental part of my mind and personality — it shapes my interpretation of most events I experience in my life."[19] Alumni single out the program's rare combination of theory and practice, with some calling for even more "real-world immersion,"[20] such as more elaborate crisis simulations.

Ironically this is one of the aspects that often draws criticism from academics outside the program, who view GS as being too vocational. They take a church and state approach, believing that scholars should study and interpret the great thinkers but not extrapolate policy or strategy from them. Practical applications are the job of people in government and think tanks, they say. In a 2013 interview in his office, then Yale president Richard Levin weighed this argument: "We don't have business courses, we have economics courses, [which] is a more rigorous approach to how the economy works. Sure, many of those people go on to business careers. But they're not learning finance, accounting, marketing tools the way you would in a first-year business-school curriculum. So the argument would be, why are we giving people preprofessional training in statecraft of diplomacy?"

Levin continued: "I think that the intellectual content of [the Grand Strategy course] is very high. It's not *doing* something vocational, it's learning about it, and it's learning about it by juxtaposing the great classics of political thought with the practical realities of contemporary diplomacy."[21]

Yale's current president, Peter Salovey, approached this question from a different angle: not whether GS is too vocational but in what ways it embodies the values of a liberal arts education. "When you talk to people recruiting for banks, for policy positions, for NGOs, but even in tech, they often say, 'We want students who can think clearly, think creatively, think critically, communicate clearly in writing and in the spoken word, who can work as part of a team, who can collaborate,'" he explained in a 2015 interview. "Often specific technical knowledge can be learned on the job, but these general skills are very hard to learn on the job. They have to be nurtured, and often the best way to nurture them is through a great liberal arts education. The Grand Strategy program . . . because of the nature of the subject matter as well as the style of teaching and because it's interdisciplinary is a great basis for learning all of the skills I just ticked off . . . It's not just the content but the way in which the education is delivered. As an educator, I'm with John Dewey in that the process of getting a great liberal arts education is the education and that the packets of content are just the vehicle by which we [substantiate] that process."[22]

With the recent creation of a Brady-Johnson professorship in grand strategy, the program is at a major turning point. Grand strategy has always been the realm of history scholars and international relations practitioners, both at Yale and more broadly. But in January 2016 Elizabeth Bradley, director of the Yale Global Health Initiative who founded a version of GS in the School of Public Health, became the professorship's first chairholder, also succeeding Gaddis as GS director. "We want this to evolve, bringing along the very best of what has been achieved but modernizing it so it stays current and flexible for developing students' critical thinking and leadership for a wider set of global problems," Bradley said of the seminar whose intellectual roots date back to Thucydides's time.[23]

Connecting to Authority

Gaddis, Kennedy, and Hill, each in their seventies, are by far GS's largest draw, and, according to students and alumni, often what they remember most about their years at Yale. Nicholas Shalek (GS '05), who took GS as an undergrad, described the course as "an unparalleled opportunity to get exposure to three of Yale's most accomplished professors."[1] A student who enrolled in GS during law school said, "I had studied [with] Professor Gaddis in college and hoped to enjoy the privilege of learning from him."[2] Jared Jonker (GS '12), who took GS while working on a dual masters degree in international relations and a business degree at the Yale School of Management, commented that GS "was honestly part of what made me choose Yale over Harvard for my graduate work. The classroom promised a dynamism rarely found even at Yale."[3]

John Gaddis, a Texan who favors tweed jackets and sensible shoes, is the world's preeminent Cold War scholar, a 2005 National Humanities Medal recipient, and the author of ten books. His 1982 *Strategies of Containment: A Critical Appraisal of Postwar American National Security Policy* is the seminal text on the post–World War II strategy formulated by George Kennan, the first director of policy planning in George Marshall's State Department. On the April 2012 afternoon that Gaddis was scheduled to lead the GS class on the Cold War, he got word that he'd been awarded a Pulitzer Prize for *George F. Kennan: An American Life*, a biography three decades in the making. The students gave him a raucous standing ovation, applauding until Gaddis abruptly turned off the spotlight. "All right," he said, "enough of that," and got back to the day's planned seminar.[4]

Excitable, slightly rumpled, and sounding like a don from Oxford, where he received his graduate education, Kennedy has an electric presence in the classroom. As one student said, "The silence . . . while Professor Paul Kennedy was speaking was the deepest I've ever (not) heard."[5] In 2014 he received the Hattendorf Prize for Distinguished Original Research in Maritime History, the most prestigious award in the field given to scholars by the US Naval War College. Kennedy is also the author or editor of nineteen books, including his best known, *The Rise and Fall of the Great Powers*, and *Engineers of Victory: The Problem Solvers Who Turned the Tide in the Second World War*, published in 2013.

Hill, who was posted to Hong Kong in the Foreign Service and then moved on to Vietnam and Israel, worked as a senior adviser to Kissinger and George Shultz at the State Department in Washington, and later for Secretary-General Boutros Boutros-Ghali at the United Nations. Opinionated and confident, he no doubt delivered his ideas to the men he served with the same penetrating stare that fixes students to their seats during office hours. As a practitioner – an expert trained in a field outside academia – Hill is a pioneer at Yale. His background as a shaper of grand strategy does not qualify him for a tenured teaching position. But he has stretched the bounds of academia, teaching a full course load – and often a double load—and being accorded the stature of a professor. In addition to authoring two books, including *Grand Strategies: Literature, Statecraft, and World Order*, he has influenced the writing of many others. At a meeting with GS students in December 2014, Kissinger acknowledged that his bestseller *World Order* "grew out of a conversation I had with Professor Hill." Hill is also the only GS professor who is the subject of a comprehensive biography.[6]

Gaddis, Kennedy, and Hill, known affectionately around campus as the Big Three,[7] the nickname given to the Allied leaders during World War II, present a united front. They're frequently asked by the university administration to make presentations to alumni and others and often consulted by Washington think tanks and strategic planners. After the US military dropped its longtime "don't ask, don't tell" policy barring openly gay men and women from serving, the professors' connections helped smooth the way for the return of the Air Force and the Naval Reserve Officers Training Corps (ROTC and NROTC, respectively) to Yale in 2012. One impetus was Kennedy's willingness to teach Military History of the West, a course that meets an ROTC requirement for Yale's cadets and midshipmen, but which has also proven to be popular with Yale's nonmilitary undergraduates.

For all of their collaboration, however—and their close, off-campus friendship—each professor anchors a different spot on the ideological spectrum, with Kennedy liberal, Hill conservative, and Gaddis in the middle. It's not unusual for one of them, usually Hill, to blurt out in class, "I couldn't disagree more!" The fact that GS students are made to decide where they fit, intellectually and politically, is an experience that most students at elite universities miss out on today, according to Deresiewicz, who taught at Yale from 1998 to 2008. "The first thing that college is for is to teach you to think," he writes. "That doesn't simply mean developing the mental skills particular to individual disciplines. College is an opportunity to stand outside the world for a few years, between the orthodoxy of your family and the exigencies of career, and contemplate things from a distance."[8]

Deresiewicz goes on to say that the real job of college is to help young people build "a self. It is only through the act of establishing communication between the mind and the heart, the mind and experience, that you become an individual, a unique being—a soul."[9] Responding, Harvard psychology professor Steven Pinker admits: "I have no idea how to get my students to build a self or become a soul."[10] But these are facets of their GS students' educations to which Gaddis, Kennedy, and Hill have given a lot of thought. "Setting aside the content and structure of the Grand Strategy program, it was the professors . . . who each individually made a profound investment and gave us an incredible gift," Eleanore Douglas (GS '02) recalls. "It was their evident and serious interest in our opinions that gave us the courage to speak. Their willingness to question their own prejudices and beliefs enabled us to begin to question ours. The valuable time that they spent correcting our mistakes and errors motivated us to seek to make fewer of them. Their unshakable belief in our abilities gave us the courage to go out and to try to make a difference."[11]

Where the professoriate is often censured for focusing too much attention on research and not enough on teaching, GS is a student-centric exception. Mentoring is a vital but mostly invisible component of the program, and the professors continue to dispense advice to former students years after they've earned their Yale degree. Talking in a Washington coffee shop between State Department posts twelve years after he took the class, Ewan MacDougall (GS '02) said, "I have pretty much never had another set of professors who took an interest in their students as much as Charlie Hill and John Gaddis. A decade out these professors respond to my email the same day. They help me think things out on a personal level. They have people over to their houses for dinner."[12]

Hill, in particular, is known for his unvarnished counsel. He'll say, 'You should do this,'" April Lawson (GS '08) said. "I don't think he means 'I have seen the future and know this is best for you.' But it's a better conversation starter than 'Well, what are you interested in?'"

Lawson checked in with him a couple of years ago after she left a prestigious management-consulting job for one in journalism. "He helped me understand how to put words to the way my career has been shaped," she said. "Hill said it's good to go from application to theory to application to theory and that this was a good next step."[13]

Hill later explained, "There's the assumption that when you leave Yale there are only four or five things you can do and only four or five places you can live. I'm trying to get students to realize that's not so. Every year I succeed in getting a student to reveal to herself what she actually wants to do. That's not something families allow. Their sons and daughters are dutiful. Then, three weeks before graduation they panic."

He told the story of a senior economics major who had applied to banking firms and law school as her parents expected. But late at night she indulged her own interests, surfing the web to learn about looted art. "She didn't know that there's an established field of cultural heritage preservation that combines law, economics, and politics until I told her about the University of Pennsylvania Museum of Archaeology and Anthropology [Penn Museum] and UNESCO," Hill said.

He added: "It's necessary to be an equal and opposite force to parents, which is new in the last twenty years. There used to be more open-minded parents. Now they're all over the students. They grind the student down."[14]

The attention doesn't always have to be elaborate, nor the advice profound. Part of what the professors offer is accessibility. Hill holds bull sessions for students on Friday afternoons. Once when Gaddis called on a student in class to comment on the Korean War, she faked her way through, confessing only later that she didn't know much about it. He gave her a copy of his book *Strategies of Containment*. "I read it, wrote down questions and reflections, and returned to his office hours for a discussion on the text," she wrote in the GS alumni survey. "I had initially felt nervous to admit to him that I had a major gap in my knowledge on his favorite time period. Yet I then felt relieved by his receptiveness and helpfulness."[15]

The reason the professors invest so much in students and alumni, especially when they could influence hundreds more students in a lecture class or thousands by teaching online, has to do with their reasons for establishing the course.

"We're not the army, we're the marine corps," a former administrator explained. "Marines are made, not trained. If you want to [turn out] the best, you can't just lecture them. You have to mentor them. We can't do that if we admitted everyone who applied . . . We couldn't keep up with people years afterward and go to their weddings."[16]

One former student related the GS model back to Carl von Clausewitz's idea of "leverage" — applying a small amount of force to make a difference. "You invest all this, and this group of people will then go off and change the world. The teaching is not the end in itself. In order to do that well, you can't take people who don't have a natural inclination to leadership. It's not making leaders out of nothing. It's accelerating that. The idea is that we'll have a community within ourselves and develop each other."[17]

Expanding the Community

In recent years the program has recruited tenured faculty to teach selected spring seminars. Before he accepted a teaching position at Columbia in the fall of 2015, this included Adam Tooze, a charismatic professor of modern German history, who was a regular guest. Other notable Yale professors who have made frequent appearances include Scott Boorman, a member of the sociology department known for his expertise on the Chinese board game wei-ch'i, Bryan Garsten, who chairs Yale's Humanities Program and teaches political science, and Beverly Gage, an expert on twentieth-century American history and the department's director of undergraduate studies, who is currently writing a biography of former FBI director J. Edgar Hoover.

Taking Hill as its model, the program has brought in additional nonresident practitioners experienced in government and journalism who can describe firsthand the constraints that often surround decision making. John Negroponte, whom Gaddis introduced as "the ambassador to everywhere,"[1] was the US deputy secretary of state under President George W. Bush and, before that, the first US director of national intelligence. Paul Solman is the longtime business and economics correspondent for *PBS NewsHour*. Besides writing for the *Times,* David Brooks is the author of four books, including the bestselling *The Road to Character,* and works as a commentator for *PBS NewsHour*. Former practitioners include Walter Russell Mead, whom the *New York Times Book Review* described as one of the "country's liveliest thinkers about America's role in the world,"[2] an editor-at-large for the *American Interest* and a professor of foreign affairs and humanities at Bard College, and Peggy Noonan, a *Wall Street Journal* columnist and bestselling author who first came to the public's attention for her eloquence as Ronald Reagan's presidential speechwriter.

Putting practitioners and scholars in the same room is unusual in undergraduate education at major research universities. Those involved cite among its benefits the potential for sparks between the professors who focus on scholarly research on the one hand and practitioners who bring their real-world experience on the other. But besides differences in experience and perspective, there's little, if any, distinction in the way the scholars and practitioners function in the GS program. In addition to coteaching the two-hour class each Monday afternoon, the practitioners preside over miniseminars on such topics as writing and economics, hold regular (and irregular! – Solman has given media training from nine thirty to eleven o'clock at night) office hours, and grade papers, creating a teacher-to-student ratio unheard of even in the most rarefied graduate seminar. At times there can be as many as five scholars and practitioners to twenty-two students in a GS classroom. "One of the tough challenges is to manage how many adults there are in the room," Brooks said.[3]

As with the full-time professors, Brooks explained, "Mentoring is in some ways the most important thing I do."

Traveling to New Haven every week from Washington, he holds office hours on Monday nights in the bar of his hotel. Once a semester he commandeers a table at Yorkside Pizza and meets with each student an hour at a time to hear about their lives. The advice he gives can be searingly personal. He helped one student cope with a parent's death and counseled another to take a job against her parents' wishes. "You owe your parents honor and love," he said, echoing Hill, "but you don't owe them your life. It's their job to get out of the way."

He also dispenses more generic advice. On whom to marry, he tells students, "You can't know, 'Will I love them in thirty years?' It's a fifty-year conversation," he said. "But you can at least answer, 'How well do we communicate?'" And on coping with life after college? "The first couple of years out of college suck," he said. His recommendation is typically grand strategic. It's the time "to widen your horizon of risk."[4]

Recruiting Students

Grand Strategy is not the most popular course at Yale. "That's the wrong category and misses the complexity of the situation," Hill said. "A popular course at Yale is when five hundred students cram an auditorium for Sexuality Studies 371: Bodies and Pleasures."[1] But while GS is not the university's most titillating class, it is among the most prominent. With an acceptance rate that averages 40 percent—it was 38 percent for the 2015 class—competition to lock in one of the seminar's forty-four spots (the size of the program doubled in 2010) is intense.[2] "Getting in was not easy and required a grand strategy of its own," Casey Verkamp (GS '09) said.[3] This exclusivity contributes to the program's appeal, especially at an elite institution like Yale where, as Deresiewicz puts it in his book *Excellent Sheep: The Miseducation of the American Elite and the Way to a Meaningful Life*, students "have been conditioned, above all, to jump through hoops."[4] One of the best ways to increase a course's popularity is "make entry to it competitive."[5]

Admitting high-caliber students means high demands can be made on them. It's what Negroponte calls "a virtuous circle."[6] It also makes GS self-selecting. At a fall briefing for prospective GSers, as students are known inside the program, about a dozen of the two hundred or so attendees left mid-session.[7] It takes chops to commit to a program that occupies

two semesters and the summer between as well as to the mas-
sive amount of reading assigned each week and a stream of
extracurricular activities. Hill's biographer, Molly Worthen,
describes the course as "the Blob" that seeps into everything
from "friendships" to "career plans."[8] It's the reason that some
students characterize GS as more a "lifestyle" than a class.[9] "It
is clear to me," Hill said, "that the desire to take the course
by the most impressive and inventive and highly aspirational
students at this university where all students fit those categories is the best evidence of its significance and power."[10]

Beyond the program's "all-star teaching talent,"[11] the
chance to be with the "smartest and most ambitious students
at Yale"[12] is another major pull. As Danielle Kiowski (GS '09)
put it: "The class format facilitated relationship building,
and discussions of deep topics taught us more about each
other than you learn about other students in other classes or
casual friendships. I felt that I knew the character of my GS
classmates."[13]

GS is one of the few Yale courses open to undergraduates, graduate and professional school students, postdoctoral
fellows, and a growing contingent of midcareer military officers. Students are selected from a range of disciplines and the
professors encourage eclecticism—Jeremy Friedman, who
became associate director in 2012 (he left in 2015 to become
an assistant professor at the Harvard Business School), successfully broadened the applicant base, reaching out beyond
the traditional channels to include undergrads in the hard
sciences and students in the Forestry School.[14] Under other
circumstances the unorthodox mix of ages, experience, and
divergent interests could potentially set up fault lines. But

some alumni said the heterogeneity was part of the program's appeal. Others said the shared language they developed in class and the amount of time they spent together, especially under the fire of the fall semester Marshall Briefs, provided common ground. "Don't forget the fellowship that comes with a small group of similarly interested students over a full calendar year. I still keep in close touch with many GSers, undergrad and grad, in and out of my degree program," a GS '11 alumnus said.[15] Laura Wheatley, the 2014 crisis simulation president, said: "As an undergrad you don't have the opportunity to have this intense experience and to [talk about it] . . . with grad students on a somewhat level playing field. It's a group of incredibly accomplished and incredibly talented people."[16] Interviewed while he was an undergrad, Ben Daus-Haberle, the crisis simulation vice president (GS '11) said: "I was expecting to walk into a class full of people with big egos. Everybody instead [was] willing to listen to each other. What I'm going to miss is not having the automatic chance to see them."[17]

Besides the ties forged in the classroom, GS alumni acknowledge the program's "unique access to senior policy practitioners," the promise of being "a way to get into high level work in Washington," and the ability to make "plum connections" they couldn't otherwise get.[18] Students' email inboxes are kept full with articles of interest from the professors, notifications of job openings and internships, and announcements of public lectures. Dinner invitations — off-the-record "*conversaziones,*" in GS parlance — are extended every couple of weeks, with Yale president Peter Salovey and GS benefactor Nick Brady; author and former US poet laureate Robert Pinsky; Canadian author, academic, and former politician Michael Ignatieff; author and former *New York Times Book Review* editor Sam Tanenhaus; Jake Sullivan, former national security adviser to Vice President Joe Biden, director of policy planning at the State Department, and deputy chief of staff to then secretary of state Hillary Clinton, to name only a few. "Network," Campbell Schnebly-Swanson (GS '13) mentioned as one of the lessons she took away from the course. "Not in strictly a professional sense. GS taught me how important meeting interesting people and simply engaging with them is to any experience. You can't just read and be tested. Meet people, cultivate relationships, and learn from their experience."[19] Verkamp also recalled a singular evening she had when representatives from the marines came to campus for a special conference with GS. "I ended up talking with one of the generals at dinner, and he awarded me one of his commemorative coins, because he enjoyed hearing about my senior essay topic, which related to military history," she said. "It was an unforgettable honor, and I was aware at the time that most of my peers elsewhere on campus who were not in GS were not having anything close to this experience."[20]

Given its small size and exclusivity, GS is often compared with another venerable Yale institution: secret societies. It's a resemblance the program perpetuates, albeit without the oath of silence or macabre rituals that come with membership in Skull and Bones or Book and Snake. At the end of their final semester, GS graduates are given a silver lapel pin in recognition of the elite fraternity they're part of. And once, in 2011, an email went out to the class advising students to dress appropriately and be prepared to meet someone important. The details were divulged only as forty-odd neatly clad young men and women boarded a bus in front of the Hall of Graduate Studies for Betts House. They were to attend Levin's and Henry Kissinger's surprise announcement that Kissinger would be donating his papers to Yale—a coup for the university given the former secretary of state and National Security Council director's longtime association with Harvard, both as a student and a faculty member. Kissinger's remarks made it clear that his decision had been strongly influenced by his close relationship with the Grand Strategy professors and his strong belief in the program. Two young lawyers—Edward "Ted" Wittenstein (GS '03), then special assistant to Levin; and Schuyler Schouten (GS '02), then Kissinger's executive assistant and a senior director at Kissinger Associates[21]—had spent a year negotiating the arrangements, on behalf of their respective bosses.

GS's prominence, and the mystique that cloaks it, inevitably lead to misinterpretations by outsiders. As one alumnus said, "GS was respected but poorly understood on campus. People knew that it was highly selective, so they were often impressed or intimidated, depending on their preconceptions. Some used it as a proxy for their indignation toward established social systems. Others reacted with humor, professing to believe that all GS students were training to be spies."[22]

But the overwhelming majority of students approach the program with a sense of intellectual curiosity and fascination with the material presented in the course. John Frick (GS '07) cited GS's "groundbreaking" method of teaching political and military history as the program's main attraction,[23] while David Gilford (GS '06) commented on the unique opportunity "to think" about the world's toughest issues.[24] "Academia has a habit of forcing people to pursue smaller and more segmented questions," a GS '11 alumnus said. "I wanted to pursue bigger, more integrated issues."[25] Others maintained that it was unlike any other course the university offers. According to alumnus Wells, the class "was the most fascinating and rigorous program I could take at Yale."[26]

Students who had been introduced to the Western canon in Directed Studies, the university's highly competitive freshman program of literature, philosophy, and historical and political thought, seemed to hunger for another course that crossed boundaries. "Students develop a passion for the interdisciplinarity and aren't comfortable later on being circumscribed by the departments and the disciplines," said Norma Thompson, who teaches DS and is director of undergraduate studies for Yale's Humanities Program.[27] Others were eager to encounter great books for the first time. "As a math and science person, I saw this as a good opportunity to round out my education," said Randall Wong (GS '11). "It exposed me to great thinkers of the past. I don't know if I would have picked up the texts otherwise."[28] A GS '14 student who took the course in graduate school said: "I love the subject material. Not only do I get pleasure from reading history but trying to learn from history — challenges, opportunities, how things have happened, what are the threads that we can pull at and learn from — so it's great that they get us studying the classics and then how . . . are [the lessons] applicable to contemporary challenges? What should we be thinking about?"[29]

Training Hawks

GS's goal, Gaddis has often said, is "to make it okay for people to be generalists again."[1] The program was on the front end of a push by some academics for more interdisciplinary courses — an antidote to ever-increasing stove-piping that has come to characterize higher education. "As departments fragment, research and publication become more and more about less and less," higher education critic Mark Taylor has written. "Each academic becomes the trustee not of a branch of the sciences, but of limited knowledge that all too often is irrelevant for genuinely important problems."[2] Gaddis added, "If you pick up the history department course listings for undergraduates, there are about 150 courses, but if you look carefully at them most will tend to be narrow. Part of the reason is that professors like to teach their own research specialties. That used to happen only at the graduate level, but it is increasingly happening at the undergraduate level."[3]

Allan Bloom addresses some of the implications of specialization in his 1987 social critique *The Closing of the American Mind*: "The net effect of the student's encounter with the college catalogue is bewilderment and very often demoralization," he writes. "It is just a matter of chance whether he finds one or two professors who can give him an insight into one of the great visions of education that have been the distinguishing part of every civilized nation . . . So the student must navigate among a collection of carnival barkers, each trying to lure him into a particular sideshow. This undecided student is an embarrassment to most universities, because he seems to be saying, 'I am a whole human being. Help me to form myself in my wholeness and let me develop my real potential,' and he is the one to whom they have nothing to say."[4]

Compartmentalization also has broader ramifications. "The [US] president, or whomever, can't be bound by disciplines," Hill added. "He can't say to himself, 'I'm only going to think about the economics of this, or I'm only going to think about the demographics or the domestic politics of this.' You've got to think about it without any fences. Everything comes at you at once . . . So you have to be multidisciplinary."[5]

Gaddis, Kennedy, and Hill try to avoid "fences" at every level, beginning with what, exactly, they mean by the term "grand strategy." "The reason why no one can tell you what it is is because it's more than one thing," Hill said. "No two of us are alike in the way we see things."[6] While the professors share the conviction that "having a grand strategy is a good thing,"[7] the course determinedly offers no formal definition, forcing students to reconcile it themselves.

The way Kennedy defines it is: "The crux of grand strategy lies . . . in *policy*, that is, in the capacity of the nation's leaders to bring together all of the elements, both military and nonmilitary, for the preservation and enhancement of the nation's long-term (that is, in wartime and peacetime) best interests."[8]

Hill hopes students "will come away having learned to

become foundationalists"—people who believe that some ideas have been proved true over time and must be assumed before other truths can be known—"but I don't think that my teaching colleagues necessarily share that," he said. "I don't think that's something they think about much. That's something I bring up. To me that's what grand strategy is. My definition of grand strategy is multidirectional, multidefinitional. You need to know what is going on here, which is extremely difficult to get people to deal with."[9]

But speaking before a group of Ethiopian government officials at Yale in 2014, Gaddis joked that his definition—"the calculated relationship of means to large ends"—is "the briefest, the most eloquent, and the most correct . . . You can wish for the stars, but your ability to get to the stars is always going to be limited."[10] He elaborated in an earlier address at Duke University in 2009: "Our knowledge of [grand strategy] derives chiefly from the realm of war and statecraft because the fighting of wars and the management of states have demanded the calculation of relationships between means and ends for a longer stretch of time than any other documented area of collective human activity."[11] Grand strategy "applies to all fields of human endeavor," Gaddis told the Ethiopian contingent. "We all have things we need and have to figure out how to get them, and that is strategy. The 'grand' has to do with significance."[12]

"Gaddis's definition is miniscule, and it's circular," Hill said. "Essentially it means don't do stupid things. If you can't reach the grapes, get a ladder. That encourages students to do what they want to do, which is to stay away from grand strategy."[13] The opposite reflex—going toward grand strategy—would be a tolerance for ambiguity. "Students have been instructed since kindergarten, 'If you do something this way, this will be the outcome,'" he elaborated. When a situation is uncertain, "they're at sea. They say, 'Quick, get me back to land as quickly as possible.'"[14] Similarly Hill believes that most people are so conditioned to think issue by issue, it's tough for them to step back to see the whole picture. "Whenever they're asked, they get jumpy and beads of sweat develop."[15]

After critiquing a fall semester Marshall Brief in which the students got stuck discussing the minutiae of the Ebola virus rather than the overall relationship of the United States with Africa, the assigned topic, Hill emailed Gaddis. "Maybe we should have some kind of joint session between now and the end of the term to go over this with them. They really don't get what GS is, even allowing for the faculty's various angles on it. We know that it's not because they lack intellectual capability; it has to be a very deep cultural-educational conditioning that puts them in a 'paradigm' . . . that they can't imagine themselves beyond."[16]

Separately, Hill said, "The area where we're successful is not this year's class or last year's. When they graduate, they don't 'get it'"—a Hill refrain. "Five years out, if they've had real experiences, then they begin to get it."[17]

When asked to define Grand Strategy, the vast majority of alumni, regardless of when they took GS, did seem to get it. They tended to cite Gaddis's definition, expounding on it to present a grasp of grand strategy as a compelling model for leadership. Some viewed the concept primarily through the lens of political power: the state's strategic assessment of economic and military priorities. As Benjamin Klay (GS '02) remarked, grand strategy is "a nation's means of achieving its clearly articulated objectives through progress that is measurable." Similarly, a GS '06 student maintained that it signals "the level of planning that focuses on domestic and international relations as they play out over the extremely long term and at the highest levels."[18]

But many graduates of the program see grand strategy as a more nimble philosophy that can guide a wide range of personal and professional decisions. "It's a way of looking on the world from an elevated position with a grounding in lessons from millennia of history behind you," one student said, adding, "It gives you the courage to take steps forward not knowing where they will lead but with the confidence that you can stake out your own course and are capable of correcting for any mistakes."[19]

"In practice, it means incorporating a sense of flexibility and appreciation for the unpredictable into one's approach to complex problems," Wittenstein, who negotiated the acquisition of Kissinger's papers for Yale, noted. Marcel Logan (GS '13) who took GS while attending the School of Management, said: "I always tell people that GS doesn't teach as much as it reveals what is already there. Some people intuitively 'get' that."[20]

Another student maintained that while "grand strategy is a perspective that allows for greater comprehension of any situation," it is for her most "closely connected to theology and the life of faith." As such, it includes "virtues such as humility and hope." She later explained that "these virtues are not merely 'nice things' or morals to practice; they are actually *the* strategy to right living. They are in accordance with the longer-term reality of the vision of God, which is also fundamentally the shorter-term reality as well."[21]

But, from a more secular perspective, Max Nova (GS '11) said: "It gave me the confidence to strike out and try something new and crazy, secure in the knowledge that Philip II [of Spain] didn't really have much of a clue either."[22]

As Gaddis told the Ethiopians, people have faced "the gap between what they hope for and what they can hope to get" for a long time. Empires have risen and fallen because of this gap. Wars have been fought and won and lost over this disparity between aspirations and capabilities. Once human beings acquired the ability to pass ideas from one generation to another then a body of experience began to develop with respect to how to bridge that gap."[23]

It's this broad sweep that GS draws on, introducing students to the field's greatest thinkers and practitioners over two and a half millennia. Starting with Sun Tzu's precepts on war, it moves briskly through Thucydides's account of the Peloponnesian War, the life of Roman emperor Augustus; Niccolo Machiavelli's recognition in *The Prince* of different kinds of morality; the contrasting leadership styles of Elizabeth I and Philip II; Carl von Clausewitz's foundational text on grand strategy; eighteenth-century philosopher Immanuel Kant's idea of peace through international order; the American founding fathers and Abraham Lincoln; European power balancers Klemens von Metternich and Otto von Bismarck; and in the twentieth century Theodore and Franklin Roosevelt, Woodrow Wilson, Winston Churchill, Vladimir Lenin, Joseph Stalin, Adolf Hitler, Mao Zedong, Kennan,

Kissinger, and Ronald Reagan. "The common thread is a search for timeless, transferrable principles," Gaddis told the Ethiopians. These seminars "are not so much telling us what to do, but creating a checklist of things to think about."[24] Or, as Wong, the engineering student who took GS as an undergraduate in 2011, summed it up: "It's like having a library of minds to apply to different situations. You can grab Clausewitz off the shelf and have him advising you."[25]

Rather than focusing on specific knowledge, the course asks students to consider how knowledge is gained, pushing them to develop an agile, adaptable intellect. Each January Hill welcomes the new class by quoting F. Scott Fitzgerald: "The test of a first-rate intelligence is the ability to hold two opposed ideas in the mind at the same time, and still retain the ability to function."[26] GS's dominant metaphor, "the opposable mind,"[27] as Brooks calls it, reaches back to nineteenth-century poet John Keats's concept of "negative capability": the idea that "Men of Achievement," as Keats wrote to his brothers in 1817, have the ability to tolerate life's mysteries.[28]

Two hundred years later the iPhone age celebrates the opposite sensibility: the idea that we have the answer to every question in our back pockets, or what Kennedy called "an explosion of data."[29] But one of GS's underpinnings is that research alone can't help us deal with pressing, complex questions: the president can't ask Siri whether or not it's in our country's best interests to send military advisers to Ukraine. Decision making isn't about looking up answers; it's about balancing a large objective and at the same time being attentive to your surroundings. In GS terminology, you have to be both a hedgehog, a person who knows only one thing, and a fox, a person who knows many.[30] Woven into the course is advice on the importance of taking first-rate notes (selectively and in longhand), of listening to hear the murmur beneath the main conversation; of seeing what others don't. One mid-September class on distinguishing "noise" from "signals"—something FDR failed to do before the bombing of Pearl Harbor—began with Kennedy saying, "If you were walking to the library on Saturday morning and happened to look up instead of down you'd have seen a thousand broad wing hawks heading to the Carolinas."[31]

It seemed like a benign opener; a random scrap of information—almost like a dust speck floating by. But it was enough to tee up Hill: "I looked out my office window about a year ago and there on a low limb in front of the provost's house was perched a red-tailed hawk. Yale students were walking back and forth underneath this hawk, and no one knew it was there. They were looking at their texts and talking on the phone." Hill continued, "This is not trivial. Consciousness is a modern thing. It's the consciousness of what is around you. What you see is a version of the signals and noise of Pearl Harbor only [more] general. What do you perceive around you? How do you read it? And what is the range of your consciousness?"[32] In a similar vein, Gaddis likened this awareness to squirrels. As he put it, "students need to be vigilant squirrels. Sure, squirrels run around, bury things, dig things up, and play with each other—but the ones that survive are aware, at all times, of the three dimensional environment in which they do these things."[33]

No matter what the animal analogy, the message is the

same: pay attention. Consider everything. Context matters.

What's being taught is "effective forecasting," Brooks said. "How do you ask questions of a situation? I think the course gives your mind more clarity. The big thing it does is scope. It takes [students] five feet off the ground and puts them at five hundred feet"[34] — like hawks.

Part Two

Looking Back

Three Views on One Problem

The Brady-Johnson Program in Grand Strategy, like many great endeavors, began over lunch. This one took place on a winter Sunday in 1998 at Kennedy's house on Humphrey Street in New Haven. Then, as now, he was head of Yale's International Security Studies Program. His guests were Gaddis, whom he'd recruited to Yale from Ohio University eighteen months earlier to fill the prestigious Lovett Chair of Military and Naval History vacated by historian Geoffrey Parker, and Hill, who'd become a full-time practitioner professor. On the conversational menu: "the state of the world."[1]

As distinct as their personal politics are, the three men found common ground that day, agreeing that Bill Clinton, then midway through his second term, seemed to lack a foreign policy vision and that their students were missing a historical context of the world.

One Clinton initiative struck the three professors as particularly wrongheaded: the push to expand the North Atlantic Treaty Organization (NATO) to incorporate Poland, Hungary, and the Czech Republic. The wars in the Balkans, which had erupted at the end of George H. W. Bush's presidency, raged on, and Russia's transition to a democracy was not as automatic as US statesmen had predicted. Along with

George Kennan, whose biography Gaddis was researching, the professors felt that expanding what had begun, in 1949, as a Cold War alliance would further hinder Russia's progress.[2] Only later did it become evident that there had been debate within the White House about the administration's grand strategy—and even whether or not it needed one. According to former deputy secretary of state Strobe Talbott, President Clinton argued that Franklin Roosevelt and Harry Truman had been given credit for having grand strategies to combat Hitler and Stalin, but in reality they'd "just made it up as they went along."[3]

After hashing over world affairs, the professors' lunch conversation turned to a new, but related, topic: where ISS was headed. Kennedy presented two options: to continue the status quo, or to rethink what they were doing and become more active. Besides his concern over Clinton's strategy gap, Gaddis was eager to find a new outlet for his scholarship. The Cold War, which he'd been studying and writing about for thirty years, was over. "I took the opportunity to suggest . . . the need to take 'crude looks at the whole,' a focus, even a program on 'grand strategy' as a way of pulling together . . . what ISS does."[4]

Kennedy and Hill liked the idea. Even before the lunch, the three men, neighbors as well as colleagues, often chatted informally about the challenges they encountered in their classrooms. "It had become clear that we had three different angles on a common problem," Hill later said. "Students who'd only been expected to work on corners of problems, gather the data, and then solve that one problem in a way that a scientist would say was scientific," but who'd never been asked to look at the whole picture or grapple with moral decision making.[5]

After he resigned from the Foreign Service in 1989, Hill had spent three years at the Hoover Institution at Stanford University in Palo Alto, California. In 1992 his wife, Norma Thompson, accepted a faculty position teaching humanities at Yale, and he received a call to work as the special policy assistant to UN secretary-general Boutros Boutros-Ghali. Donald Kagan, a preeminent Yale professor of classics and scholar of the Peloponnesian War, asked Kennedy to find an intellectual home for Hill.[6] Kennedy named him a diplomat in residence at ISS, a made-up title that came with an office, a box of business cards, and an invitation to teach a seminar on the United Nations for international studies majors. The gig also brought "friction from other faculty members"[7] over what they saw as Hill's "right-wing" bent, Kennedy said.[8] This grumbling didn't bother Hill, who commuted from New Haven to Manhattan on weekdays, returning early on Monday afternoons in time for class. But he was shocked to find how little his International Ideas and Institutions students—all seniors—knew. "They didn't have any idea what the United Nations did," he said. "They knew nothing about its history. They didn't know what had happened to create the need for international law, or what international law was."[9] At Stanford he'd designed a continuing education course called Statecraft, basing the syllabus on current events, "but not in the way people think of current events." Instead, he approached it from a foundational perspective: "Where did the Arab-Israeli conflict come from? What are the intellectual origins of it? What are the great minds that bear upon it? What is the source of Zionism? I could get people to see that underneath any current problem there are reasons why it's the way it is. Those reasons are, in most cases, connected to ideas and they go way, way back. Sometimes they're bad ideas. But if you don't know where the ideas come from, you don't know why certain things are done."[10]

At Yale, Hill revisited some of the same questions with his seniors, revamping the class to be more like Statecraft. Kennedy was so pleased with the results that he asked him to expand the seminar into a yearlong lecture course required for all sophomores majoring in international studies.[11] By 1998 Hill had not only been teaching the seminar for several years but had become a regular instructor in the Directed Studies program for freshmen, teaching Historical and Political Thought, and Literature.

Kennedy, too, liked Gaddis's suggestion of giving ISS a broader portfolio. Because it was self-funded through foundation grants and reported only to the provost, ISS was agile enough to take on what he called "outside, fifth-wheel ventures" that the political science and history departments, with their more rigid structures, couldn't accommodate. Kennedy had underwritten the research of a PhD student who had gotten access to the Red Army secret archives of the Stalin period. He'd agreed to host a group of scholars from United Nations Studies, which moved to a different university every three years (this happened before Hill came to Yale and was unrelated to his work). From 1993 to 1996 the Ford Foundation, coincidentally, gave Kennedy and Yale a $1 million, three-year grant to study America's new role in the United Nations after the Cold War, a project to which

Hill offered informal, but invaluable, advice. To Kennedy a course on grand strategy would be consistent with ISS's self-styled mission as "an incubator" for any undertaking related to international and security issues, "usually historical, broadly defined, nonideological, and not too big or too dodgy."[12]

The intellectual void the professors recognized was comparatively new. As Hill often asserts, people used to know what grand strategy meant "in their bones."[13] According to Lawrence Freedman in his book *Strategy: A History*, the ability to strategize is so fundamental it predates humankind. "Deception," coalition building, and "the use of violence" — all rudiments of strategy – can be traced to chimpanzees. The Hebrew Bible is filled with stories in which the protagonists put elements of strategy to use: David, for instance, relied on surprise and sureness to slay Goliath.[14] "We assume that a kind of grand strategic logic has existed for as long as people have had to match up unlimited aspirations with limited capabilities," Gaddis added. "Sun Tzu and Thucydides are the earliest records of this logic that have survived, but they certainly didn't invent it."[15]

While strategizing predates history, the term "grand strategy" didn't catch hold until the early nineteenth century – the result of the large-scale expansion of warfare during the Napoleonic era. After touring military schools in France, two leading West Pointers, Captain Sylvanus Thayer, who became superintendent, and Dennis Hart Mahan, a professor of military engineering, introduced the theories on war and strategy espoused by Antoine-Henri-Jomini and Carl von Clausewitz into the US Military Academy curriculum.

Mahan's teaching and writing, which integrated "French theory with emphasis on American common sense," influenced a number of Civil War generals, including George McClellan, Ulysses Grant, and William Tecumseh Sherman.[16] Reflecting on his wartime experience in an 1887 article in the *Century*, then the nation's best-read magazine, Sherman popularized the notion that grand strategy encompasses all aspects of war. In the four decades after the Civil War, a time of explosive growth in America, grand strategy became such an everyday concept that people regularly evoked it, even when they talked about nonmilitary topics, including agriculture, industry, and the country's burgeoning railroads.[17]

The idea of grand strategy recrossed the Atlantic in the early years of the twentieth century in its original military context, gaining favor among professors at Oxford and Cambridge. Calling their group the "Round Table," its members sought to glean lessons on leadership found in ancient Greece, promoting their thoughts in articles and monographs. Although the Round Table died with the decline of the British Empire, B. H. Liddell Hart, a distinguished twentieth-century military theorist, refined the concept of grand strategy (Kennedy was his research assistant from 1966 until Hart's death in 1970). And with Kennan's idea of "containment," the United States continued to be guided by an overarching strategy through the end of the Cold War.

But by the cusp of the twenty-first century, both the phrase and the consistency it promoted had been relegated to the archives. In the political realm grand strategy had been replaced by what Hill likes to call "tiny strategy" — a series of one-off initiatives with no connective tissue, such as Bill Clinton's call for school uniforms and V-chips for TVs in his 1996 State of the Union address. And university classes that dealt even obliquely with anything grand strategic – the uses of power or the history of empires – had all but been abandoned, a casualty, the professors said, of 1960s' social tumult. Hill, who graduated from Brown in 1957, received a broad, classical education that enabled him to expound comfortably on the differences between the Renaissance and the Enlightenment on his Foreign Service exam. Ten years later the exam no longer tested applicants' grasp of intellectual history but of current culture, such as name the director of *The Graduate*. According to Hill, "That was what people in America knew."

In the 1960s, he continued, "Wherever you looked the overwhelming demand and assumption were that whatever existed had to be torn down. Question Authority! The curriculum was an authority, so tear it down. American Literature had a canon! Get rid of it! Skull and Bones – tear it down! In fact, tear down Yale! You were supposed to deal with issues that were immediately in front of you. No longer were you supposed to teach the high realms of international politics. No one knew any history. My joke was that [students] could tell which came first – the First World War or the Second [World War] – by studying the titles of things."[18]

Kennedy, likewise, blamed the wide neglect of international security on the "memory of and hostility to the Vietnam War. Anything that had to do with power and imperialism and empires and foreign policy had got us into trouble," he said. So when the old guard retired, scholars who specialized in more topical areas, such as gender or environmental history, replaced them.[19]

Writing in the *Wall Street Journal*, Peter Berkowitz takes a similar view, attributing the disappearance of military affairs courses from elite institutions partly to "the same post-Vietnam hostility to all things military that impelled faculties and administrations to banish ROTC from campus[es]."[20] When the article was published suggesting that that the ideal military affairs course would start with Sun Tzu and Thucydides, Gaddis was exultant. "That's not a military history course," he said, correcting Berkowitz. "That's a Grand Strategy course. [Berkowitz's] rationale and justification for it could have been written by us . . . I was accusing Charlie Hill of ghostwriting it."[21]

Beginning in the mid-1970s, when college campuses began to represent the broader population, so, too, did their course catalogues. But in the prior years it wasn't only military-inspired classes that suffered. In his book *The Marketplace of Ideas: Reform and Resistance in the American University*, Louis Menand reports that except for the scant time between 1955 and 1970 when college enrollment jumped dramatically, the percentage of undergraduates who walked away from their commencement ceremonies with a degree in the liberal arts had been slipping steadily since the early twentieth century. He highlights the role the Cold War played in shifting the emphasis of universities, especially the fear set off by the Soviets' 1957 launch of Sputnik and the subsequent passage of the 1958 National Defense Education Act. Ideology had already been edged out at the end of World War II, replaced by widespread interest in scientific-like research to address social ills. But, for the first time, rivers of federal money began flowing directly into American colleges and universities to shore up science and foreign languages, along with a call for heightened scientific rigor.[22]

Whatever the causes for the near disappearance of diplomatic and military history, the most damaging effect was that by the 1990s there were few professors who could actually teach it. That's when Kennedy began using ISS as a "greenhouse to protect the plants," turning out "an astonishing number of newly minted PhDs."[23] This made Yale, and ISS, the ideal place to launch a grand strategy program.

Seated around Kennedy's dining table, it was immediately clear what the professors *didn't* want: Gaddis, Kennedy, and Hill weren't interested in establishing another think tank. The Grand Strategy course they envisioned wasn't meant to copy, or compete with, the John F. Kennedy School of Government at Harvard or the Woodrow Wilson School at Princeton, which focus on current policy.

Nor were they looking to Yale's past for a model. From 1935 to 1951 Yale's Institute of International Studies had a commanding role in shaping international policy, influenced by noted nuclear strategy expert and Yale professor Bernard Brodie and William T. R. Fox, best known for coining the term "superpower."[24] But after Alfred Whitney Griswold replaced Charles Seymour as Yale president in 1951, he dissolved the institute — and every other university program that smacked of practicality, including the School of Education — sending the institute's director, Frederick Dunn, and several professors packing to Princeton. Griswold was "a devout believer in the humanities and a militant foe of vocationally oriented disciplines and specialists," Jerome Karabel writes in his book *The Chosen: The Hidden History of Admission and Exclusion at Harvard, Yale, and Princeton*.[25] Jeremi Suri explains in *Henry Kissinger and the American Century* that unlike Harvard, which became the leading Cold War university, Griswold wanted no "blurring of the lines between academic and policy analysis . . . scholarship and national defense."[26] Nor would he have been any more accepting of the current Grand Strategy program. Gaddis recalled: "We were pretty well convinced that if we were to do [GS, it would be] a classics-based course . . . that would pull together the great classical works and then in some way to try to relate them to current issues"[27] — a twist on the great books that some critics see as too vocational and that Griswold would likely have found abhorrent.

But dipping into the Western canon makes GS part of a long tradition. Writing in 1869 British poet Mathew Arnold championed studying "the best that has been thought and said" in the world. "Arnold's hope was that through the classics readers would overcome their 'stock notions,' or ill-formed and rote assumptions," writes Tim Lacy, the author of *The Dream of a Democratic Culture: Mortimer J. Adler and Great Books Idea*. It wasn't until three decades later, around 1900, that the University of California at Berkeley became the first American university to offer a great books course. In 1917 John Erskine, an author and English professor, proposed a similar class at Columbia, but the faculty initially rejected his plan, partly because "A great book couldn't be read in a week — When is [a student] to eat and sleep?"[28] (Former GS students admit to having had the same problem![29])

The forerunners of Columbia's two-year core curriculum, adopted in 1920, began after World War I to provide "young people from different backgrounds" – mainly Jewish immigrants – "with a common culture," Menand writes. Colleges "looked at the world, and at what they perceived to be at stake in current events, and they decided that there were certain things students needed to know that most of them were not getting from specialized study."[30] Mortimer Adler and Robert Hutchins had a slightly different view of the great books' value when they began their famous program at the University of Chicago in 1930. Theirs was an attempt to overcome the same fragmentation and vocational fervor that the GS professors, and higher education critics, complain about today.[31]

Using the great books to study, and make, grand strategy also has illustrious published precursors. Edward Meade Earle's *Makers of Modern Strategy: Military Thought from Machiavelli to Hitler*, an essay collection published in 1943, "immediately became the single most influential primer on grand strategy for American wartime and postwar planners," Gaddis has explained.[32] One reader was Kennan. In 1946, when he was brought to Washington from the US embassy in Moscow to design the curriculum in grand strategy at the National War College, the first coursework of its type at an American educational institution, he relied heavily on Earle's abridged version of Clausewitz's *On War*. Kennan took particular note of Clausewitz's theory about the "center of gravity." Because offensives outrun their supply lines, only minimal effort by defenders can swing the momentum around psychologically and lead to a retreat. Kennan also cited Tolstoy, who gives Clausewitz, a Prussian general, a cameo in *War and Peace.* "His point was that Stalin is Napoleon," Gaddis said. "Napoleon went East; Stalin went West. But Stalin wound up, in 1946, with half of Europe, just as Napoleon wound up, in 1812, with a third of Russia. But now what? What do they do with it?"

The Western canon's effect on Kennan reached beyond the War College curriculum. Having read Edward Gibbon's *The History of the Decline and Fall of the Roman Empire* on multiple transatlantic flights during World War II, Kennan had absorbed Gibbon's proposition that "nothing is more difficult than to attempt to hold indefinitely in thralldom than conquered provinces." Kennan concluded that if the United States could find a way to apply pressure in the right place, it had the possibility of shifting the balance away from Stalin at a minimal cost. "That indeed is where the idea of the Marshall Plan came from," Gaddis concluded — "from Clausewitz, Tolstoy, Gibbon, and the great books."[33]

Other statesmen also made practical use of the classics. George Marshall said that no one could understand the Cold War without having read about Athens and Sparta in Thucydides's *The History of the Peloponnesian War.*[34] As a young PhD student Kissinger included the book in his International Seminar at Harvard, an interdisciplinary summer course for up-and-coming policy leaders created in 1951 by William Yandell Elliott, the dean of the Harvard Summer School. And after Admiral Stansfield Turner became president of the Naval War College in Newport, Rhode Island, in the early 1970s, he made Thucydides the introductory text for the Strategy and Policy course,[35] which enrolls mid-career military officers. The curriculum went on to cover other classical works, including Clausewitz and West Point's Mahan, plus historical cases and contemporary issues.

Gaddis experienced Turner's curriculum firsthand. In 1975 after the acclaimed publication of Gaddis's first book, *The United States and the Origins of the Cold War, 1941–1947,* the admiral invited him to become a visiting professor. Then in his midthirties, he was younger than his students. The Vietnam War had just drawn to a close, and emotions were raw. "People [who had fought there] were realizing Vietnam would be regarded as a military failure," Gaddis said. Turner made Thucydides's *History* compulsory reading, a revolutionary idea, given the book's distant era. No explanation followed. "I was literally reading it two days ahead of my class," he said. "It was quite a desperate thing. I was wondering why we were reading it. The students were wondering why."[36]

Then Gaddis understood.

"There were no [contemporary] books we could use on Vietnam that were not incendiary," he explained. "No one wanted to talk about their experiences. [You can] use the classics to open up something you can't talk about normally. It became cathartic," he added. "Some of the same processes that had brought the Athenians to Sicily had brought Americans to Vietnam."[37]

Reading the classics, Gaddis continued, is "a very old idea, yes, but old ideas stay around, because they have value for new situations. That's why the classics don't go away . . . whereas the latest theory may fall apart in a few years, like Tom Friedman's [assertion that] there's never been a war between countries that have McDonald's[38] or Francis Fukuyama's 'The End of History?'[39] The classics hold up better. They're adaptable."[40]

The lunch that took place in Kennedy's dining room resulted in an ambitious Grand Strategy work plan. The first item was to draft a "What Is Grand Strategy" essay-manifesto. In keeping with his role at the State Department under Kissinger and Shultz, Hill took the initiative. In a memo to his two colleagues, summarized by Worthen in her Hill biography, he commented that "the expectations of policy-makers and political scientists expressed at the end of the Cold War had all proved egregiously wrong . . . the wonks had promised that Boris Yeltsin's Russia would align itself with the United States; that the 1991 victory against Saddam Hussein in the Gulf War would evolve into lasting security in the Middle East and peace between Arabs and Palestinians; that the end of the superpower bipolarity would revivify the United Nations. What had gone wrong in their thinking, to account for such errors? Even more worrisome was that so few seemed to notice the glaring incongruity between reality and the world order they had predicted." [41]

A few weeks later, the Hill memo, with Gaddis's and Kennedy's input, evolved into a letter they sent to leaders in academia, journalism, government, and business. Noting that "particularists" were now in charge of policy-making, the letter, which Worthen sums up, argued that "these people . . . have difficulty seeing the entire thing. They pigeonhole priorities, pursuing them separately and simultaneously, with little thought to how each might undercut the other.

They proceed confidently enough from tree to tree, but seem astonished to find themselves lost in a forest." This would become GS's foundational language.

Decrying the lack of "great generalists in positions of authority," Worthen writes, "the letter presaged a debate that's popular today."[42] "Once upon a time, humanists taught great texts and raised big questions," Anthony Grafton and James Grossman comment in the *American Scholar*. "Their courses might have lacked a certain specificity, but they had a soul. And nobody worried in those days about whether those courses led to a job. According to this narrative, in the past half-century or so humanists have tried to become specialists, as if they were scientists — or pretending to be."[43]

It sounds like Hill talking about students' studying "corners of problems."[44]

Eminent Responses

B y July 1998, the framework for a Grand Strategy curriculum that would teach "across space . . . across time . . . [and] across disciplines . . . with a heavy reliance on outside presentations by practitioners"[1] had gained enough momentum that Gaddis and Kennedy met with Kissinger at the Brook Club in New York in hopes of getting his blessing. They presented the class as "a long-term effort to shape the minds of future policy-makers, not as something that would have any immediate impact," Gaddis wrote in his journal. Kissinger "immediately picked up on this theme. There was no hope of having any influence on anyone in the policy community or on the verge of entering it, he said. He mentioned, in this connection, George W. Bush, who he says is already too preoccupied with raising money to think about what he might do if he should become president."[2]

Gaddis and Kennedy mentioned the NATO expansion debate as the precipitating event, but Kissinger viewed the expansion differently. He believed that Russia would never become a democracy, and that it already had too much power in NATO. But he agreed that President Clinton had bungled the expansion. "It all emphasized the importance of our initiative, we helpfully commented, and he nodded approvingly."[3]

If the professors needed further proof that the Clinton administration was muddling through, they received it that fall. A team of high-ranking staff officers from NATO headquarters in Brussels spoke at Yale to make the case for expansion. During the question period, a political science professor raised his hand. Had the briefers considered how Russia would regard such a move? Perhaps enlarging NATO would undermine President Boris Yeltsin's efforts to democratize the country, or even drive the country into a new alliance with the Chinese.

"Good God!" one of the officers exclaimed. "We'd never thought of that!"[4]

That reply, Gaddis would later say, "pushed Paul, Charlie, and me into thinking that, if nobody had a grand strategic perspective at such high levels, we'd better get going with what we'd only been talking about, up to that point, at Yale."[5] They'd already scheduled a weekend conference for November 1998 to tackle two questions: Could grand strategy be taught? And if so, how? Gaddis, Kennedy, and Hill invited *New York Times* columnist and author Thomas Friedman, a handful of people from the Brookings Institution, McKinsey & Company, and the Council on Foreign Relations, and a dozen fellow professors and graduate students from Yale and other universities, including one of the world's foremost historians on twentieth-century Europe, Zara Steiner, from Cambridge, England. They were to meet at the Boulders Inn, a rambling, shingled, Victorian-era mansion in Litchfield County, Connecticut.

On the first night Kennedy chaired a discussion on the most successful and unsuccessful historical figures and what could be learned from the past in appraising contemporary grand strategies. It was "not too satisfactory," Gaddis noted in his journal, "with everyone sitting around in soft armchairs dozing off after a good deal to drink and a heavy meal."[6] Those paying attention, however, got a preview of some of the underlying lessons that would later be embedded in the spring seminar. One, which comes up in the class discussion on the founding fathers, is the idea that grand strategies are forged at turning points, hammered out when leaders are under pressure. Gaddis would later quote Samuel Johnson to make this point: "Depend on it, sir, when a man knows he is to be hanged in a fortnight, it concentrates his mind wonderfully."[7]

The weekend conference, according to Gaddis, picked up momentum on Saturday. He chaired a session with Friedman, an engaging thinker and speaker, whose real-world examples and focus on economics provided the right counterweight to the historical emphasis of the previous evening — and to Gaddis's viewpoint. "Where Gaddis saw a political scene with no urgency, Friedman saw an economic scene in crisis," one note taker at the conference wrote.[8] Friedman's main thrust was that globalization was happening quickly, and no one was minding the store: CEOs and hedge fund managers were shaping foreign policy more than the State Department.

In the afternoon Hill talked candidly — "more than I've heard him do," Gaddis wrote — about his experience as a grand strategist working for Kissinger and Shultz.[9]

The concluding session, on Sunday morning, began with Gaddis's depiction of what the professors saw as a destructive phenomenon in higher education: undergraduate and

Teaching Common Sense

graduate students were being "whipsawed between the general and the particular," he said. "There is a better way to educate them . . . we need some time to remind students of . . . what it is to have a sense of strategy—that is, how the parts to relate to the whole."[10]

The conference culminated with Kennedy sketching out, on the back of an envelope, a yearlong program—he called it "a diploma"—in Grand Strategy. The first semester had a familiar ring: it would stress qualities of mind rather than immediate future policy, looking at the leadership styles and sets of principles that guided strategists through history. The writings of Thucydides, Clausewitz, and other classic works would be used to prepare students to deal with unknown

DIPLOMA IN GRAND STRATEGY (at I.S.S.)

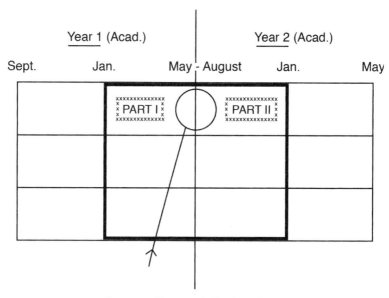

Summer Research Project (team project)

issues. This part would be taught in the spring so that professional-school students would be free of their first-semester requirements. Despite Gaddis's, Hill's, and history professor Donald Kagan's urging to include undergraduates, Kennedy's program was designed solely for grad students. The summer would consist of individual research projects, with the fall semester set aside for student presentations. It was the first time these disparate components were linked together (the crisis simulation was added in 2002). What emerged was a course that was simultaneously old-fashioned and groundbreaking.

"I have not seen anything like it," confirmed Peter Richardson, the president of the Smith Richardson Foundation, one of ISS's main funders at the time.[11]

"It was like doing a Lego piece," Kennedy said. "It just clicked into place. We realized we had it."[12] The professors returned to New Haven well pleased with their progress. "The whole [conference] had been intended as a preliminary consideration of the problem—does it exist? Can it be fixed? We concluded, I think, that the answer was 'yes' on both counts," Gaddis noted.[13]

But his private musings also underscore the tentative nature of the undertaking. "Where we go from here," Gaddis wrote, "isn't quite clear."[14]

First Year

After the Boulders conference Gaddis and Kennedy guided their embryonic Grand Strategy program through Yale's bureaucracy, having breakfast with different deans, selling it as a graduate seminar with ancillary lectures for undergrads. But "the truth," Gaddis lamented in February 1999, "is that it's all pretty vague still," a fact that Will Hitchcock, then associate director of ISS, who became a history professor at the University of Virginia, pointed out "in a dead-on memo about smoke and mirrors."[1]

In June, despite Gaddis's uncertainty, Caroline Lombardo, who had graduated from Yale College, worked with Hill at the UN, and been a Marshall scholar at Oxford, arrived to take up her post in a newly created position: special assistant to the Grand Strategy project (she'd also attended, and taken notes at, the Boulders conference). Her job was to develop the GS course syllabus, which Kennedy had largely left to Gaddis to figure out. "I was aware again of how little solid thought, either on my part or Paul's, has actually gone into this," Gaddis confided in his journal. "It's the old problem of not being able to tell very clearly whether I'm being platitudinous or profound; also the other old problem of trying to skate too easily over too much thin ice intellectually, without doing the really hard work that's required here."[2] There was an air of excitement and anticipation along with the doubt. Lombardo spent time with each professor in his home library, taking books off shelves. Each picked out readings critical to his thinking and professional development that still form the backbone of the syllabus today. Although Hill hadn't yet signed up to teach the seminar, he claimed primacy over Thucydides and Kant, Gaddis over Clausewitz, and Kennedy over histories of British and European statesmen: Salisbury and Bismarck. "The professors were giddy," said Lombardo, who called them "the boys" behind their backs.[3] Hill surprised Kennedy and Gaddis in October by announcing he'd like to come onboard to coteach. "This is great news," Gaddis wrote, "and makes the whole enterprise more viable than if it should just have to depend on the two of us."[4]

The professors, Lombardo, and Ted Bromund, who replaced Hitchcock as ISS's associate director and also helped shape the program, used the Thanksgiving break to select the first students. They were looking for top-notch candidates with an interest in grand strategy, career aspirations undergirded by social value rather than greed, and a sign of potential leadership. Gaddis pronounced the sixty or so applications they received "very gratifying," from which the committee settled on twenty-four students—including, surprisingly, given Kennedy's earlier insistence on grad students, six Yale College juniors.[5]

Then the curtains opened, and the show began.

"Over to 31 Hillhouse [Avenue] for an orientation meeting of the Grand Strategy seminar, with twenty-four very excited bright-eyed students, only slightly rattled by the size of the syllabus we were smacking them with," Gaddis noted.

"Paul did most of the talking, pulling out all the stops to say, in effect, that the eyes of Yale, the nation, the world, the known universe, were on this seminar."[6]

The first-year class met in the intimate setting of Alwin Hall, an old clapboard house converted to office space used by ISS, next door to the Yale provost's residence. It was a heady time. One professor usually led the Monday-afternoon session, while the others sat in back, frequently turning to Lombardo, who was taking notes, to say, "Change this part," or "Put down that I disagree with this," as though she were Herodotus, recording for the ages. On the one hand the professors emphasized the ancient arts of reading, writing, and thinking, no matter what technological advancements may occur in the future, and on the other, a "let's give it a try!" anything-goes attitude.[7]

The professors didn't intend for the seminar to be Socratic in nature, Hill said, "but it immediately took on those characteristics, with a dialogue, or trialogue, among the three over every text and issue, conducted in a rational, critical, civil, and ironic, often sardonic, style that made the discussion come at whatever topic was before us from three different angles, quickly recognized by students as left, right, and center, something not done in universities. And, Socratic-like, we never came to a conclusion; the basic question was unanswered by us and put out there for each student to work out individually thereafter if possible."[8]

Though unintentional, the approach forced GSers to wrestle with the course's core principles. It wasn't always comfortable. But the value became apparent immediately, particularly for the Yale College juniors. As Gaddis and

Hill predicted, admitting undergrads made for a dynamic mix. Undaunted by the tower of reading assignments, they proved not just the equals of the postgraduate fellows but often outperformed them.[9] The younger GSers posed many of the most searching and penetrating questions, while, according to Hill, the postgrads handed in some of the least reflective papers. This drilling down tapped into the original role of the university as a place for young people to develop ways of thinking and skills for life before being launched into the world—what Deresiewicz calls building "a soul."[10] Lombardo said: "The notion that if you don't give your brain that space as a young person, when are you going to do that?"[11]

Hill likes to point to the younger GSers' success as proof that Yale College graduates, unlike undergrads at most other colleges, shouldn't be required to get a graduate degree, an idea that reaches back to the mid-nineteenth century, when a four-year liberal arts degree was an end in itself and not merely a preprofessional chute. "Most American colleges are inadequate and not much more than uppity forms of high school, so graduate work is needed as remedial education," he said. "But not so for graduates of Yale. It is a form of foolishly imposed servitude to insist that Yale College graduates go on to get, e.g. a 'Master's' degree in international relations at someplace like G[eorge] W[ashington] just in order to be promotable later on some Washington career ladder."[12]

In its first year GS was less strictly focused on geopolitics than later events forced it to become. The United States wasn't at war, and the economy was roaring. Nearly every week a guest from an arena that required thinking grand strategically, including the corporate world, was invited to class. Then the group would head to Mory's, a private dining club on York Street, for dinner. The dinners became a core part of the program.

In those days Mory's, which opened its doors in 1849 when Zachary Taylor was in the White House and enjoyed its heyday sometime prior to 1960, was down at the heels and resisting modernization. The menu still offered Welsh rarebit and Baker soup, a house specialty, and the music was provided by Yale's a capella groups. The all-male Whiffen-poofs, founded at the club in 1909, sang there every Monday night (as they still do). While the GS gang could probably have sung the Whiffenpoofs' repertoire by heart, the dinners added sheen to the program. "They really felt that they were part of something much larger than a course," Lombardo said.[13] Scott Kleeb (GS '00) recalled these informal din-ner conversations with guests, often followed by drinks at Gaddis's home, usually at the invitation of Kennedy, as he walked his dogs, as "the skimmings of an already rich cream."[14]

But where the spring semester was a successful, kinetic experiment, the fall was, by many accounts, including the professors', lackluster. Gathered around the conference table with their students, Kennedy and Hill (Gaddis spent the 2000–01 academic year in Oxford) gave too much time over to discussing "What I did during my summer vacation," and the assigned readings seemed "arbitrary," Bromund said — especially in comparison to Thucydides, Machiavelli, and Kant, which had been taught in the spring.[15]

Gaddis, who was gentler in his criticism, nonetheless

agreed. "The first year," he said, "was just okay, but not exciting enough that I was persuaded that this would be a long-term prospect."[16] Having planned a year-on, year-off schedule, the professors didn't have to decide immediately what they would do in 2002.

The 9/11 Effect

The terrorist attacks on September 11, 2001, changed everything, including the Grand Strategy program. It was, as the *New York Times* editorial board wrote the next day, "one of those moments in which history splits, and we define the world as 'before' and 'after.'"[1] Nearly everyone on the Yale campus showed up at a candlelight vigil held the night of 9/11, but that did little to assuage the sadness, bewilderment, and fear students felt. "We were all worried about how our classes were going to go," Gaddis said. Rick Levin called a series of impromptu faculty meetings in the president's office at Woodbridge Hall to figure out how the university could best respond. Sitting at a table with two dozen other professors, Gaddis raised his hand. "Students are perplexed," he told Levin. "Maybe we could organize a series of lectures and discussions that would give direction to the campus."

According to Gaddis, Levin said, "Whatever it takes. And by the way, you're running it."[2]

"Levin was looking for professors to be able to speak and write on the events and the animosity that lay behind them, but no department could get itself organized; they couldn't move fast enough," Gaddis said. "There was a vacuum. That's when ISS earned its reputation as a place you can go when you need to get something done quickly" — a campus quick reaction force.[3]

Gaddis persuaded Cynthia Farrar, a lecturer in political science and director of urban academic initiatives,[4] to help. Together with input from students, they created a series called Democracy, Security and Justice: Perspectives on the American Future, which brought in speakers once or twice a week over the course of the 2001–02 academic year. They included not just luminaries such as Gary Hart, the former senator who had cochaired the bipartisan Commission on National Security/21st Century for the US Defense Department, which in January 2001, had predicted an attack such as occurred on 9/11, but also gave Yale students the opportunity to grapple with the issues at hand. The main focus of the talks was, How do we adjust to our new lives in which everything is familiar and different?[5] or, as Gaddis also phrased it, how "do we keep hope alive?"[6] A *Yale Daily News* editorial pushed students to think deeply about their role in the world: "The calling of our time is the war against terrorism. A new generation of Yale graduates now faces the world with a duty and a purpose."[7] As if in response, a rising junior and soon to be a member of the 2002 GS class, stood at one of the Democracy discussions and announced, "I love this country. I love this place. I love what we're doing here tonight. I love it so much that I'm prepared to defend our right to do it . . . which is why I'm joining the Marines. It's people like me who make it possible for people like you to be here doing what you're doing."[8]

It was an off year for GS, and, in that void, the Democracy series became a proxy for the class, addressing questions that might have come up in the comfortable informality of Alwin Hall had GS been in session. At one Democracy planning meeting, at Gaddis's house, another student (also GS '02) asked the key question, "Would it be OK now for us to be patriotic?"[9] With so many students seeking answers, demand for the course shot up, particularly among undergrads. As one program administrator said, GS "slid into this open space at the university that no one else was filling."[10] Two months after 9/11, when the professors accepted applications for the 2002 program, they were inundated. GS was onto something.

Gaddis, Kennedy, and Hill reconfigured the fall semester, building in four weeks on the current national security environment followed by the murder boards. They also introduced a primitive end-of-the-semester crisis simulation game, a precursor to the more sophisticated one they now run. The fall had the heft it had been missing. "I was so excited by the first classes," an alumnus said. "Remembering it now gives me chills. It felt like being ushered into some special room to have the secrets of the world unlocked. And that kind of happened. Well, sort of. It at least gave some insight into how things outside of academia operated at a time when I had no idea. It was very exciting to come to class to hear what other people would say. I liked that we had different viewpoints, that people disagreed very comfortably and openly about pretty serious ideas."[11]

When the course ended the following fall, Hill, Gaddis, and a couple of friends were sitting on the porch at Hill and Thompson's house. Kennedy was on sabbatical in England. "We can't wait a year to do this course again," Gaddis told them. "We have to do it immediately. There has to be a 2003 course."

Hill looked at Gaddis. "Yeah," he said. "That's right."[12]

GS has been taught every year since.

Brady and Johnson

Yale's significance in Nick Brady's life as a student, from 1948 to 1952, was double sided. On the one hand, in the immediate postwar period in which Brady and Charlie Johnson ('54) attended, there was a clear moral ethos of what it meant to be a Yale man, with its emphasis on public service, graciousness, and gentlemanliness—qualities they took into adulthood and exhibited throughout their careers in business and government. On the flip side, there was the Yale that William F. Buckley Jr. criticized in his seminal 1951 *God and Man at Yale* for being anti-Christian and anti-capitalist. Buckley singles out a professor, Ralph E. Turner, whose wildly popular history course, Contemporary World—which Brady took as a junior, in 1951—was "emphatically and vigorously atheistic," he writes. "An able scholar, he is nevertheless a professional debunker, a dedicated iconoclast who has little mercy either on God, or on those who believe in Him, and little respect for the values that most undergraduates have been brought up to respect."

Buckley goes on: "Many Yale students laugh off the influence of Mr. Turner and ultimately classify him as a gifted and colorful fanatic. Others . . . are deeply disturbed by Mr. Turner's bigoted atheism."[1]

Brady fell into the latter category. It wasn't so much Turn-

er's atheism that he found repellant. It was what Brady, looking back on his undergraduate years more than six decades
later, called Turner's "excessive moralizing." As Brady writes
in his memoir, *A Way of Going*: "One day [Turner] made
the stark point in a lecture that the only difference between
Communism and the Catholic Church was that Communist
prison camps were here on earth. I can still remember being
jarred by that view."[2]

In the decades after graduation, Brady was only superficially involved with Yale. Captain of the championship 1952
squash team, he became engaged by the global potential of
the sport, contributing generously to the new Brady Squash
Center and, subsequently, to a leading researcher at Yale
Medical School working to combat ovarian cancer. Johnson,
a close Brady friend, gave a substantial donation to renovate
the Yale Bowl (and, as mentioned earlier, would go on to
underwrite the Johnson Center for the Study of American
Diplomacy, which supports research in the Kissinger papers,
and to become among the largest single-gift donors in Yale's
history, for the construction of its two new colleges). In
the early 2000s, when Rick Levin asked Brady to consider
another gift, Brady told his friend Sam Chauncey, former
assistant to Yale presidents Griswold and his successor,
Kingman Brewster: "I would give more money to Yale if it
had something to do with common sense."[3]

The idea of sound judgment has always resonated with
Brady. After his father (Yale '29) died in 1971 he briefly considered creating a Yale professorship in his memory. When
one of his father's friends asked what department it would
be in, Brady answered, "I'm not sure, but I know what he

was long on — common sense."[4] During the younger Brady's career at Dillon Read and Company, and as a US senator and treasury secretary, he'd repeatedly come into contact with people who had made all A's in college but who couldn't hold down a job; people, in short, lacking in common sense. He gravitated toward the opposite: grounded people such as Kissinger, George Shultz, and Johnson, who had kept Franklin Resources on an even keel for more than fifty years. "If an idea passes Charlie's muster," Brady often says, "you know you're on the right track."[5]

The relationship between common sense and the academic community isn't an obvious one. By definition, a liberal arts education is about pursuing knowledge for its own sake, without a practical application.

But Chauncey got a two-thousand-watt idea.

"Having attended several GS classes, at some point common sense popped into my head," he said. Chauncey got Gaddis's permission to invite Brady and Johnson, who, coincidentally, had met Gaddis and Hill at various Yale events.[6]

While common sense had never been an explicit part of GS's phraseology, Brady and Johnson found much in the program to like. The sparring among the professors from different points on the political spectrum, which forces GSers to reckon with their core values, leaves no room for a Ralph Turner. Yet while GS lacks the didacticism that Brady found so off-putting during his Yale years, the syllabus's focus on the classics, the personal attention the professors give their students, and the course's emphasis on public service were comfortably familiar — a throwback, even, to his time at Yale. "From the First World War through the Second into the

'60s, Yale had just an amazing record of producing extraordinary people who went into national service — the military, intelligence agencies, and other parts of government," Rick Levin said in 2013. "And there had always been in . . . each generation from the First World War through the 1960s a number of faculty who had always believed this was part of their mission to educate people for those public service roles. And many, many outstanding men — they were all men until '69 — were attracted to those callings and inspired by the example of a number of these professors. We fast-forward to the 1990s, and we didn't really have that . . . we still talk about service as part of the ethos of the place . . . but there weren't those role models of faculty who were really explicitly hoping to educate their students for national leadership. Paul Kennedy and Charlie Hill and John Gaddis conceived this idea in that old tradition."[7]

Brady and Johnson recognized another plus: in giving Hill, a practitioner professor, equal stature to the scholars, GS didn't play by the rules. This unique set-up so impressed them that in 2006 they decided to endow the program, specifying in their gift papers that their support was predicated on maintaining parity between scholars and practitioners. "The scholar is immersed in the work of conducting research, and then relating his or her findings through teaching and writing. The practitioner learns to manage the interactions of people and resources to achieve goals and provide leadership in society," the papers state.

They continue: "Students will benefit immensely from the interaction that can occur when the scholar and the practitioner teach together in the same classroom. As

professors, practitioners and students examine problems
and issues from the perspective of history and research, on
the one hand, and actual experience, on the other, wisdom
will be the result."[8] Part of the Brady-Johnson endowment
has been used not just to retain Hill, the original practitioner
professor, but also to bring in the others: Negroponte, Solman, Brooks, and previously Walter Russell Mead and Peggy
Noonan.

Levin has since confirmed that GS's innovative use of
practitioners "inspired" him "to see that there was even more
potential in this approach," and it became his model for the
teaching of contemporary global affairs when he set up the
Jackson Institute of Global Affairs in 2009.[9]

So what about the connection between GS and common
sense? "We never thought about it that way," Gaddis con-
ceded, "but it's perfect. It really does come around to what
we're trying to do, which is to equip young people to deal
with an unforeseen future . . . Common sense is like a foreign language. There are all kinds of ways that you can use
it."[10] GS always comes back to foxes and hedgehogs, which
is not unlike common sense. Speaking to a group of visitors
in 2014, Gaddis melded the two ideas together: "You will
see that the Yale campus is filled with young people walking. They all know where they're going but they're not looking out in front of them but at their hand . . . texting each
other. It's amazing that they can do this without running
into each other. This skill while walking—I hope not while
biking or driving—is an example of holding a hedgehog idea
while being attentive, like a fox, to surroundings. Common
sense—you know where you're going when you're crossing

the street but jump out of the way of a bad driver—operates at the level of ordinary life, although not necessarily at the level of responsibility. That's something we need to confront. How can we teach the agility these students show and transfer it to higher realms of policy making?"[11]

The answer: by looking to the past, at people like Augustus and Elizabeth I, who showed a lot of common sense, and people like Marc Antony and Philip II, who did not.

Yale and Beyond

In 2006 when Nick Brady and Charlie Johnson endowed the Grand Strategy program, they hoped it would become a model, quickly spreading beyond grand strategy's historic roots in war and statecraft to other parts of Yale and the academy writ large — or, to put it in author Malcolm Gladwell's words, to reach a "tipping point."[1] It didn't need to be an exact copy of GS. Nor could it be, as everyone involved understood. Other universities that picked up the idea would have to adapt the course to their own circumstances, capabilities, and needs. Kennedy often compared its expansion to Benedictine monasteries, each having autonomy but still belonging to the order of Saint Benedict.[2]

It turned out they didn't have to go far.

Elizabeth Bradley, then associate professor of public health and director of the Health Management Program at the Yale School of Public Health, and the GS professors had never met. It took Chauncey, who'd preceded Bradley in her director position and understood both GS's potential for the public health sphere and Bradley's entrepreneurial spirit, to make the connection. But soon Bradley was crossing the campus each Monday afternoon to attend the GS seminar. She saw the relevance for her field immediately. "I became enamored of the big principles they were teaching, such as 'be prepared for friction,' and 'see the big picture but also see the thing in front of you,'" she said in an interview. "At the end of each class, I would walk out and say, 'Wow! That is exactly how we need to think in global health.'"[3]

In 2010, with Brady-Johnson seed money, Bradley started Strategic Thinking in Global Health, a one-semester version of GS for twenty-six students, evenly split between undergrads and graduate students. Like GS's original Big Three, Bradley and her coteachers, Leslie Curry, a public health scholar, and Michael Skonieczny, a practitioner, had substantial differences in perspectives on their field. Bradley's skills are quantitative, economics based, and appreciative of the market; Curry's are qualitative, political science based, and appreciative of the force of regulation. Skonieczny worked in Washington for a decade as a lobbyist on global health legislation and understands the reality of making change in a field crowded with conflicting ideas.

Before long it was Gaddis and Hill who were crossing the campus, heading to the School of Public Health as Bradley's guest lecturers. Strategic Thinking students aren't made to pore over the great books like those in the parent class but instead to absorb principles such as "start with the end in mind," "take an ecological approach," "recognize that tactics matter," and "integrate timely intelligence and data into health interventions and improvement efforts." "We talk about 'friction' and 'paradox,'" Bradley said. Like military and diplomatic strategy, there are also foxes and hedgehogs in global health. "There's a major fault line over whether to use vertical funding, i.e., by disease, or horizontal funding — well coordinated health delivery systems for all, irrespective of disease, such as doctors and nurses, clinics, hospitals, community health workers, and ministries of health," she added. "You can't do both. No one has enough money. People who are horizontal are more fox-like, whereas hedgehogs focus on a single disease, such as HIV."

Bradley continued, "Students have to be thoughtful and see themselves as part of a long stream of history lived through a collective voice as opposed to the dominant, single leader standing above the dead bodies all around. It's so hard, because our [cultural] reality is that when things go wrong you usually can find someone at the center of it, and we say, 'What a terrible leader!' But that explanation is insufficient. It's obviously much more complicated and involves the context."[4]

Strategic Thinking students are also put through the paces of Marshall Briefs. "The issues are big," Bradley said, offering China and the Environment; Strategy for the Gates Foundation Over the Next 20 Years; and Mental Health in Afghanistan as examples. "When they leave," she said, "they should know how to design a good strategy and how to present it."[5]

Approaching disciplines through a grand strategic lens is novel, and important pedagogically, Bradley said, because typically universities "create ideas, and then we stop. But to see those ideas manifested; to move those ideas out into the world—that's what Grand Strategy picks up. I don't think the academy always thinks that's its responsibility, but we can at least prepare students to do this better."[6]

Besides Brady and Johnson, another person who saw potential in GS was philanthropist Roger Hertog, president of the Hertog Foundation. Soon after hearing Kennedy speak, in 2007, he offered to fund scholars interested in establishing their own grand strategy programs, many of whom he met at a 2008 weekend GS conference sponsored by the Brady-Johnson Program. Thanks in large part to Hertog, versions of GS are now taught at about a dozen other major civilian universities, public and private, including MIT, Tufts, Columbia, Bard, Princeton, Temple, Johns Hopkins, and Georgetown, on the East Coast, Duke in the south, and Carnegie Mellon, the University of Texas at Austin, the University of Chicago, and the University of Wisconsin at Madison in the Midwest, as well as at West Point and the Air War College. Asked about his attraction to the program in a 2015 phone interview, Hertog explained, "If you're really looking for young men and women to have a leadership capability, they need more than training. They need knowledge, they need history, they need an understanding of decision making and how leaders go through the agonizing process of becoming great leaders . . . Leaders in the political-diplomatic realm in the course of hundreds of hundreds of years [have a] common set of denominators: first and foremost a tremendous amount of courage; the second would be an incredible persistence. They're willing to live through things even under adversity to continue forward. Third, they have a few big ideas. They aren't scattered. They don't have fifty things they think are important, whether it's Mr. Lincoln or George Marshall or Ronald Reagan or Margaret Thatcher or Stalin. Leaders aren't all good people. These things usually take longer than anybody recognizes. Things don't just happen overnight, because you're a smart person and you're willing to do it. That's what it looks like in the history books. You actually learn those characteristics in different ways in [GS], and you gain a deep perspective."[7]

But during the conversation Hertog explained that he'd found the Brady-Johnson Program difficult to replicate and had since changed tactics, instead offering intensive, short-term institutes on discrete topics in fields such as political science, economics, and war studies. One factor that makes the Yale course unique is the combination of professors, whom he called "enormously creative. It's very rare in the academy to find people who are so entrepreneurial," he said. "There are very few programs in the academy that will try to marry philosophy, some literature, history, strategy, decision making. They put that together, and it [takes place] over a year, and it's grueling, and in the interim they're actually bringing up great leaders to meet with these [students.] That's a very rare thing."[8]

The financial resources behind GS also make an enormous difference, he said. Most grand strategy courses are taught by one professor over a single semester. "Do I think other schools could do this?" Hertog asked. "The answer is yes, but it's hard. You have to buy [the professors'] time." He added: "The genius — the missing elixir — is the Brady-Johnson grant. This is really hard stuff, and at the heart of it is this unique contractual relationship that Nick Brady and Charlie Johnson were able to negotiate with Yale. If Brady and Johnson had done nothing else in their lifetime this is a real testament."[9]

Part Three

Looking Forward

Making It Memorable

The forty-two students assembled in the sleek amphitheater of Yale's Maurice R. Greenberg Conference Center seem nervous. The first steps in being admitted to the Studies in Grand Strategy seminar — making it through the required essays, faculty references, transcripts, and face-to-face interviews to test how well they present an argument and respond to questions and counterarguments — are over. But the course they are now embarking on will be demanding. The spring semester moves through twenty-five hundred years of history in thirteen weeks. In the fall, the students work in teams to present an assigned, and usually unwieldy, topic, as if they're briefing bosses who demand near perfection. As Kennedy described it, "We just throw the bloody furniture at them."[1]

But that wouldn't start for a few weeks. This was orientation — often the first time the "younger strategists," as opposed to the "elder strategists" from the outgoing class, who also get invited, meet the professors and one another. "Tell your life story in thirty seconds," Gaddis tells the undergraduate, graduate, and professional-school students who sit facing him. "Make it memorable."[2]

Seated in the neat rows of desks that make the Greenberg Center look like a small-scale UN General Assembly, the students introduce themselves one by one. "I'm very interested in diplomacy and Foreign Service, and I see this class as a great way to look at this," Brandon,[3] a junior ethics, politics, and economics major from Los Angeles, says, starting things off. "I'm involved in the Yale College Council."

"I would say you run the Yale College Council," Gaddis replies, urging the council president on to less humble heights. "And you left out the best part."

Brandon hesitates. "I also do opera, and I have been directed by Professor Gaddis's wife."[4]

Class hasn't even started, and the GS professors are pushing the students hard. This is the first of many times during the program that they'll be asked to speak extemporaneously. If their performances aren't as smooth as one might expect of a future secretary of state, they will be after the two rounds of murder boards and the crisis simulation in the fall. Allison Collins (GS '10), who took GS as an undergrad, recalled, "The program demanded that you present your perspective thoughtfully, intelligently, and with an openness to questions and criticism. Put more simply, I had to stand up for myself and for my right to be in the room. I wasn't always successful, but I got better at it as we went along." She added, "I think the Marshall Briefs are amazingly useful for anyone who wants to go into any profession that requires any communication whatsoever."[5] Amira Vallani (GS '09) maintained that learning "to formulate opinions and articulate them, even in front of well-known or well-respected figures, including visitors,"[6] was one of her chief takeaways from the program.

The emphasis on eloquence is one aspect of GS that harks back to an earlier, classical education, when young men were taught to declaim. "The two things Lincoln and FDR had in common was oratory: the ability to give great speeches," Gaddis told a visiting delegation, singling out two US presidents whose grand strategies are studied during the course.[7] As Charlie Johnson said, "Great leaders have great communication skills."[8]

The professors make clear how such skills can be cultivated. In 2011 the press secretary in the crisis simulation placed his laptop next to him as he began his morning briefing and started googling answers to the reporters' questions. He didn't get far before being heckled. "Can't you conduct a press conference without your laptop?" one of the professors shouted from the audience.

"No," he replied, "I'm of the younger, electronic generation."

The professors walked out, and the president quickly replaced his press spokesman with another who could answer questions without the benefit—or curse, as the professors would say—of technology.[9]

Growing Cherry Trees

GS places the same importance on writing as it does on speaking. It's a class where clarity and brevity are prized. "In terms of careers, life is nothing but a series of term papers whether you're going to be in government or business or in law" (or just about any other job that involves a desk, he could have added), Hill said at a required writing workshop held early in the semester. He singled out poor structure as a frequent problem: "There's no logic chain that's one, two, three, four that can carry the reader along." Gaddis added, "Think of the way a cherry tree grows. It grows from a seed, a small sprout, a trunk, leaves, and then fruit. There's a logical sequence. It all has to happen in a certain order before the fruit can drop." The other way is cherry picking. "Oh, that's a nice cherry. Here's another. Just serve them up, wherever they came from, to your teacher."[1]

Imprecision and carelessness are also judged harshly. A paper that hasn't been properly revised or proofread is "like running cross-country without any sprint at the end," Hill told the new GSers, as Gaddis handed out a writing checklist giving examples that he's collected from student papers. One entry is called "Big Words: Some students (and professors) believe that using lots of $8 words when a few 25 cents ones would have done just as well enhances their credibility. As in: 'Optimizing the efficiency with which ingredients required to produce beverages deemed desirable prior to participation in soporific seminar discussions are utilized is to be commended.' Translation: 'Don't waste coffee.'" Another is "Elegance: Think of whatever your ultimate standard of gracefulness is—whether a Mozart concerto or a DiMaggio swing or a (Groucho) Marx put-down or Virginia Woolf's description of the first Queen Elizabeth (in her novel *Orlando*, pages 22–23)—and then ask with respect to everything you write: 'could I at least come a little closer to that?'"[2] The checklist "should be right next to your laptop or to pen and paper," Gaddis told the group. "Every piece you hand in you should check against this. Like the checklist an airplane pilot would have before taking off. That's why you don't want to fly on certain airlines these days. The same thing happens to Yale writing."[3]

Scott Kleeb, who took GS as a graduate student, said that GSers need only look to the syllabus for inspiration: "The Peloponnesian War lasted some twenty-seven years, and was fought amongst dozens of city-states and related empires on a then-global canvas . . . and Thucydides describes it in only four hundred some-odd pages. If that's not distilling key elements from immeasurable inputs, I don't know what is."[4] There's a second method of teaching revision: Gaddis shows (he says, "subjects") GS students early drafts of his own manuscripts. But these lessons are just fine-tuning. The students have to be serviceable writers to be accepted in the first place. They also need to be engaged in the world around them.

Back in the amphitheater, the new students are rattling off their credentials. Alex, a junior in Ezra Stiles College, double majoring in global affairs and political science, is interested in national security policy in South Asia and the Middle East, focusing on the peace process. In California, where he grew up, he founded a nonprofit to help school districts launch student evaluations of teachers' programs. Now he teaches health education in the New Haven public schools, serves on the board of a Yale service organization, and runs a technology company with clients such as National Pubic Radio (NPR) when not studying modern standard and Egyptian colloquial Arabic.[5] Caitlin, a junior, who took the past semester off to trek around Patagonia, is concentrating on religious studies and statistics. She performs in campus musical theater productions, runs freshmen outdoor orientation trips, edits the *Yale Historical Review,* and participates in a computer-coding workshop. Dexter, an air force officer and first-year law student, speaks of his fascination with microfinance. Adam, a Yale College economics major, talks about his interest in the intersection between the economy and "major issues like global warming."[6]

Brandon later adds that his predecessor on the Yale College Council had told him he'd be crazy to take on any extracurricular activities besides student government, where he manages fifty-five people. But he ignored the advice. He is a campus tour guide, a member of a prestigious a capella group, and spends his "downtime" rehearsing for *West Side Story* "instead of sitting in front of a TV," he said. He is also taking GS. "I enjoy having my hand in a lot of things."[7]

Standing on the dais beside Gaddis, Hill is preparing to set these students straight on what he considers to be *the* cardinal sin in American higher education and the country generally: his "tiny strategy."[8] "We in America have been moving away from anything that resembles grand strategy, so that socially, anthropologically, everyone is conditioned not to understand it," he says. The "rise of the social sciences," has created the sense that "we're here on earth to solve problems."[9] Instead of studying leaders, he says, students are now driven by issues such as the environment, population growth, and human rights. "But they don't know the history of these issues." This is a lack. "We do things because of ideas and institutions. The ideas and institutions are already there when we walk into them . . . You have to know where they come from. They come from every direction. You have to consider everything."[10]

Using History

This work—instilling the habits of thinking broadly and strategically—begins even before students return to campus in January. For 2015 the reading assignment over winter break included Freedman's 751-page tome, *Strategy*; Isaiah Berlin's article "The Hedgehog and the Fox," based on a fragment of Greek poetry that says: "The fox knows many things, but the hedgehog knows one big thing"; and an essay by Winston Churchill, "Painting as a Pastime," on the hobby that gave Britain's World War II leader a respite from the world stage and enabled him to see what lay in front of him, including water and light, in new ways.[1]

Churchill must have been onto something. After Gaddis recommended the essay to George W. Bush, the former president took up a paintbrush of his own. He rendered dozens of portraits of dogs before moving on to likenesses of world leaders, including Russian president Vladimir Putin, Jiang Zemin, the former general secretary of the Chinese National Party, and the Dalai Lama.[2]

Few of the readings have this immediate impact, but, as Brooks said, "You can't be a cabinet secretary without a thoughtful bookshelf. The people in Washington who get promoted are not just functionaries. About half have had contact with all this stuff."[3] While the spring course syllabus can vary slightly from year to year,[4] the books, drawn primarily from the Western canon, emphasize the foundations of the nation-state and the international system that are the basis of statecraft. During the semester, students are asked to plow through Sun Tzu's *The Art of War;* Thucydides's *The History of the Peloponnesian War;* Machiavelli's *The Prince;* Kant's *Political Writings;* Hamilton, Madison, and Jay's *The Federalist;* and Clausewitz's *On War.* The supplemental readings include Plato's *The Republic;* Plutarch's *The Lives of the Noble Grecians and Romans;* Hobbes's *Leviathan;* Gibbon's *The History of the Decline and Fall of the Roman Empire;* and de Tocqueville's *Democracy in America.* And there's a smattering of Virgil, Tacitus, Augustine, Locke, Rousseau, Adam Smith, Hegel, Nietzsche, Marx, and Tolstoy thrown into class discussions. The material is what gives GSers, as Brooks put it, "a better ability" than most students, even those at Yale, "to step back and look at the grand sweep."[5]

The syllabus, which claims to represent "the best thinking and writing" on strategy,[6] is as notable for what it doesn't include as for what it does. The ongoing conversation about multicultural representation has been sidestepped. While science, religion, mythology, psychology, fiction, and drama come up in class discussions, they aren't required reading, although, as Gaddis noted, "We couldn't possibly do Augustus without talking about Virgil, or Elizabeth and Philip without referencing Shakespeare, or Lincoln without Whitman and Twain—and the most frequently recurring dilemmas in class come from Berlin's article on Tolstoy (foxes and hedgehogs) and F. Scott Fitzgerald's opposing ideas simultaneously held."[7] In his book *Grand Strategies:*

Literature, Statecraft, and World Order, Hill writes, "The great matters of high politics, statecraft, and grand strategy are essential to the human condition and so necessarily are within the purview of great literature." Even Jane Austen's *Emma,* he writes, possesses "a dimension wholly apt for statecraft—in Emma's case, the gathering and misanalysis of intelligence."[8]

The spring syllabus continues: "We expect you to extract a set of principles for the making of grand strategy that will be useful in any future leadership role in which you may be called upon to connect desired ends with available means."[9] Starting in the alien settings of ancient China, Greece, and Rome and taking students up to present conflicts and threats, the professors drive home certain guiding concepts that they believe span both time and circumstances. As Thucydides said of his *History,* these readings are meant to provide "knowledge of the past as an aid to the understanding of the future, which in the course of human things must resemble if it does not reflect it."[10] When the students are themselves decision makers, the big thinkers will still be in their minds—"a hedge," Gaddis claims, against the day when "they'll be too busy to take our phone calls or track our tweets."[11] Solman adds, "The idea is to get [students] to internalize" the insights, "not to spout them. If it was just a checklist, it doesn't have the emotion. But if you remember what happens to Thucydides and you were moved by it—you tussled with it—then you will have made it your own, even if you reject it."[12]

The principles include the role of national character (Thucydides); patience (Augustus); the recognition of a dual morality, one to save the soul and another to save the state (Machiavelli); personality and decision making (Elizabeth I of England, a nimble fox, and Philip II of Spain, a dutiful hedgehog); leverage, proportionality, so that only as much force as necessary is used, and allowing for unpredictability (all in Clausewitz). Gaddis, Kennedy, Hill and the other professors cite the American founding fathers as proof that adversity breeds creativity. And they speak of Lincoln as an expert in sequencing: having an internal compass but knowing when to deviate from it and how to return to it.

The notion that history offers lessons to steer present-day actions resonates with alumni, a majority of whom cite the first portion of the program, when they study the great works, as the most valuable component. Many mentioned specific principles, including "the ability to understand [a] situation at all levels and focus on the appropriate level at the appropriate time"; "the military is an extension of politics"; and "Ask 'so what?' 'Then what?'"[13] In class the professors refer to this as "the dog and car syndrome": dogs chase cars but don't know what to do when they catch one. As Sibjeet Mahapatra (GS '12) explained, "Expecting and planning for the inevitability of things NOT going according to plan" — friction — "has been fundamental to my ability to succeed in the highly speculative world of technology."[14]

Other former students discussed the value of the classics as a whole. Ewan MacDougall said that GS gave him "the entire trajectory of developments between then and now" and "a real appreciation for the values we have enshrined in our government today . . . It also gave me a sense that these things are not to be taken for granted. They are fragile."[15]

Campbell Schnebly-Swanson said the readings taught her that "history is very much like an empirical database stretching back and delivering us all the examples we could need to organically estimate . . . what is best to do today. There really are eternal truths, and especially in human nature/politics."[16] Danielle Kiowski, who, like Schnebly-Swanson, took GS as an undergrad, said, "One aspect of the value of reading great works of strategy is that it provides one with context in which to view current situations. The human experience today is much the same as it was in ancient times, just with fancier machines. Works of grand strategy, like fine literature, familiarize the reader with people — their beauty and their follies. This allows the strategy student to escape the confines of his own thinking. He sees variations in how people have approached events similar to the one that he faces and is better able to anticipate the choices that they will make."[17] Likewise, Sebastian Swett (GS '11), who took the class while in law school, said: "History, even ancient history, is never so distant from our present day. I had never read classics and I assumed they would be dry, stilted and hard to understand because, well, they were old. I was wrong. I loved reading all of them and found them incredibly relevant to our current world."[18]

Part Four

A Class in Four Acts

Act One:
Spring Classics

Rooms 217B and 220B of the neo-Gothic Hall of Graduate Studies, with their small leaded glass pane windows that filter the wan winter light, walls the color of lightly browned toast, exposed pipes overhead, and old-fashioned chalkboards, have all the charm of a church basement. But this is the high pulpit, where statecraft is taught with near-religious zeal.

Since 2010 when the class size nearly doubled from about twenty-two students to around forty-two, the GS seminar has met in two groups, Athenians and Spartans, named for rival city-states in ancient Greece. During week one the Athenians take up Sun Tzu's *The Art of War*, written circa 500 BCE — a cornerstone text that set the stage for Asian and European thinking on grand strategy — while the Spartans discuss Thucydides. The next week they trade, leapfrogging through the syllabus until the two sections come together in April for several classes, including Democracy vs. Totalitarianism, The Global Economic Order, and Grand Strategy of Insurgency. The semester ends with a joint class on the Cold War.

The Art of War has a distinctive place in GS as the course's only acknowledgment of any classical tradition outside the

West. A compact military text for Chinese generals, kings, and emperors on how to wage war, it is written as maxims, such as "The worst policy is to attack cities. Attack cities only when there is no alternative"[1] and "You should not encamp in low-lying ground." Some scholars contend that despite the book's title, Sun Tzu, a contemporary of Confucius, was influenced by the spiritual thinking of his day, which promoted harmony and peace.

"If you have to wage war, what's the best way?" Gaddis asks.[2] The students, seated around an oak seminar table with their names on placards set before them, stay quiet, their heads down, willing themselves not to be called on. Finally one gets the courage to speak. "Quickly," he says.

"Through nonviolent means—alliances," another answers.

"The best way is to not wage it at all," ventures a third.

Bingo.

More Mr. Chipping, the beloved boarding school master from *Goodbye, Mr. Chips,*[3] than Charles Kingfield, the Harvard law professor who terrorizes his first-year students in *The Paper Chase,* Gaddis tosses out questions to get students involved in the discussion, not to embarrass them by revealing what they don't know. The approach could be called the "Socratic method lite." "My philosophy in teaching a seminar is that it's got to be spontaneous," Gaddis later explained. "It can't be a lecture, and yet it's got to have some structure. I will have . . . about five points I want to get through, but I want the students to think they've thought of each of the five. What I'm doing is trying to set something up so that one will make the point, and then I can say,

'Ah, that's the Daus-Haberle principle.' It sticks with them more."[4]

This is what happens at the beginning of one session on Augustus, when a student, Kate, fires off the opening question: "When we're talking about grand strategy, are we talking about something inherent in the text or in hindsight are we placing it on the text?"

Gaddis smiles. "What the class has just witnessed is an act of theft," he jokes, "because you have stolen my opening line. Would you like to run the class?"[5]

One year during a joint session on the Cold War, he made good on his invitation, and let the students conduct the class. "I'm never sure how to run the discussion on the Cold War, because I worry that I'll say too much, and thereby stifle spontaneity," Gaddis explained. "So I'm always experimenting." That time he called on a student with no warning and asked her to begin the conversation. When she ran out of things to say, she handed off her role to a classmate, who then appointed his successor. "We had five or six students in front of the class over the next couple of hours," Gaddis recalled. "I encouraged them to use the blackboard to illustrate their points, in the Charlie Hill manner. By the end of the class they'd filled one wall and run over onto the other one, but the diagrams each of them put up bore no connection to what the others had left there. So I was able to turn this into [another] lesson on the difference between cherry-picking and cherry trees growing: we had cherries in a bowl, so to speak, but no logic chain linking them. None of this was planned, but some of the best class moments aren't."[6]

Gaddis takes a similar improvisational approach with his coteachers. "We don't plan ahead of time," he said. "We don't have to work out a scenario of who's going to do what." Whereas many professors talk about "my course," the GS professors can't. They share the stage, with no effort toward making their teaching styles uniform. Differences of opinion and hectoring one another aren't just professorial shtick but an essential part of the course's pedagogy. As Solman said, "It's a course that likes sparks."[7] Gaddis said, "Charlie and Paul [Kennedy] and I have known each other long enough that we can tease each other in front of the class. The students love this. You have to know someone pretty well before you can pull that off. That's one of the things that's unusual about the class. Few courses have multiple professors and even fewer can disagree publicly."[8]

In 2003, before the war in Iraq and his appointment as a GS practitioner, Solman was reporting on the prospective cost of the war for the *PBS NewsHour*. Yale professor Donald Kagan suggested that he focus on GS "because there would be disagreement," Solman recounted. He staged a debate, as Gaddis explained in class one day, "with Hill, predictably, for the war, and Kennedy, equally predictably, against it. I, judiciously, tried to evaluate the pros and cons of each position."

"Also, predictably," he went on, "Paul and Charlie made it onto TV, and I wound up on the cutting-room floor. Let that be a lesson to all of you!"[9]

Contrary to this example, however, the professors don't always take a fixed position. There are times that Kennedy and Gaddis argue from a scholarly view and Hill interjects a dose of reality, saying, "It didn't happen that way!"

"It's in the archives!" Gaddis and Kennedy say.

"But I was there!" Hill retorts.

Room for disagreement among the professors extends to the students. "GS is subversive," a former program administrator commented. "It challenges the orthodoxy that the professor is right 100 percent of the time. We train students to challenge their professors."[10] Brooks concurred. GS, he said, "puts you in a room where certain things are debated. The students come and talk to me about the class. I'm always impressed that they praise and criticize it. They have advanced views of what happened in that two-hour period. It's not just a body of knowledge that gets dumped down on them. It's a conversation. They inhabit a method of thinking. It's a worldly thoughtfulness."[11]

"This is a seminar," Hill tells the students in a class on Thucydides, "but it isn't purely a seminar. We want as much back and forth as we can get, but there's so much material to get through it's going to be more of me lecturing."[12] As Worthen explains in her Hill biography, he's also "known for striding over to the chalkboard to scratch out three words and a triangle and pronounce, 'This is Thomas Hobbes,' or reduce *The Peloponnesian War* to a six-part logic chain." Students' notebooks "are filled with [his] thought trees and idea charts."[13]

Today's class is no different. "We've jumped way ahead to get to Renaissance Italy," he says, leading off a session on Machiavelli as he draws an isosceles triangle on the board representing the end of the Middle Ages.[14] "The main point from our perspective is this is the start of the modern world. *The Prince* is considered to be the start of modern politics.

We'll try to figure out today why that is. It's coming off the late Middle Ages. People stood at the bottom of the triangle and looked up to God at the top. The farther you were from God the less power you had. The church would be closer to God and you as an individual were not . . . Suddenly when we're in Renaissance Italy, power is otherwise. Not that this original view is gone, but power is horizontal, and it is up for grabs. It's out there, and if you know what's good for you, you'll grab some, because the old, medieval view is breaking down. So all around you it looks like chaos. It's not as hierarchal as it was before."

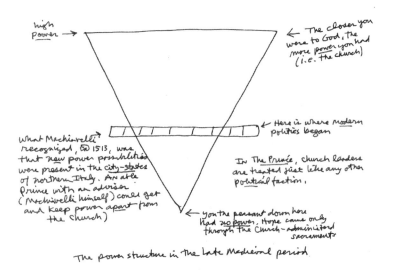

The power structure in the late Medieval period

"It looks like you'd better scramble and get going because if you don't get power, power is going to get you. This is modern."

Hill teaches the course in a "come to Niccolo way,"

Solman later said. "It is 'you people don't get it—it's a brutal world out there. This is what Machiavelli teaches you. Live with it.' Otherwise, it was just too pat."[15]

Solman, the business and economics correspondent for the *NewsHour*, has interviewed more than fifteen thousand people during his forty-plus-year journalism career. Besides introducing economics and opera (he plays Mozart's *Marriage of Figaro* during the Adam Smith workshop) into the course, he saw his role in the Machiavelli class as Hill's foil. "I would say, 'You're telling them this is okay? Borgia did what?'" He was referring to the actions of Cesare Borgia, the duke of the Romagna, who put the relentlessly cruel Remirro de Orco in charge. Remirro successfully stabilized the lawless province, but the people despised him. To win them over, Borgia had Remirro's body cut in half and left in the town square beside the bloody knife.[16] The lesson is that a "clarifying act of violence," as Hill calls it, if precisely aimed, can save lives.[17]

Where Hill's classes march students deftly through the terrain of select politics, culture, religion, literature, and history, Kennedy's are a ramble—a Sunday stroll—with stops for ruminations on questions such as, "If a Martian asked you how the little place became the big place, how the Roman Empire sustained itself from the first century to the fourth century, the answer is: it was organization." Kennedy is also irreverent.[18] A clip from *Monty Python's Life of Brian* is a perennial feature of his seminar on the Romans. "They've bled us white, the bastards," one rebel leader says. "They've taken everything we had, not just from us, from our fathers and from our fathers' fathers . . . And what have they ever given us in return?" The men call out different answers until he's heard enough. "All right, all right! But apart from better sanitation and medicine and education and irrigation and public health and roads and a freshwater system and baths and public order . . . what *have* the Romans done for *us*?"

"Brought peace," another character says.[19]

Adam Tooze's teaching style is semiautomatic rifle. He shoots questions and comments at students and fellow professors, and, as he intends, they shoot back, making the seminars he runs feel unnervingly like hand-to-hand combat. In a class on authoritarian regimes that Tooze cotaught with Kennedy and Solman, a student argues that Stalin was a better grand strategist than Hitler.[20] "Stalin is more totalitarian; Hitler's more authoritarian," the student says. "It makes Hitler's strategy ineffective."

"There's not a single decision re steel allocation not signed off on by Hitler," Tooze says, dismissing the student's perspective.

Kennedy jumps in. "If it were possible to think of steel as a key element in the early twentieth century, in which other regimes do leaders sign off on this essential thing? Is that an indicator about control?" he asks.

Another student responds: "One of the things we've gotten a sense of is which was better, democratic or authoritarian regimes."

"The Great Depression was the real killer," Tooze says. "It's not politics; it's economics."

"When you see a state where the choice is lying low versus adopting a messed-up grand strategy, doesn't this go back to Bismarck?" a third student asks.

"The national character variable is doing a lot of work

for you," Tooze answers, referring to Bismarck. "A party that's never won has more than 30 percent of the vote seizes power, and turns the country into a one-party state. That's not national character. It's national policy formation."

"National character is a theme of this course," Solman says, "In 1933 the Nazi Party gets 44 percent of the vote. That's more than Clinton in 1992. In 1932 37 percent may not be kickass, but it's clearly a plurality. The largest party appealing overtly to patriotism doesn't garner more than 37 percent. It means it's a heterogeneous society."

Turning to Tooze, Solman goes on: "So you find the stereotype of Germany believing it has a unique culture is not the story for you at all?"

"Germany," Tooze slings back, "is a fruitcake. It's so incredibly rich."

As the Sun Tzu class continues, students are instructed to remember the acronym CAT, which stands for "complete," "accurate," and "timely" — the triad of principles behind successful intelligence gathering.[21] *The Art of War's* impact has grown in the twentieth and twenty-first centuries, according to Scott Boorman, the sociology professor who has cotaught the Sun Tzu seminar. "Increasingly," he said, "the emphasis in the military is less on blowing things up and more on information dominance — knowing more than the enemy; and knowing more, more quickly."[22]

In GS students are able to view the theoretical and the practical, the past and the present, side by side.

"I have a question for Professor Negroponte," (it's a hallmark of GS that *all* of the faculty, whether scholars or practitioners, are called "professor") Gaddis says. "As former and first director of national intelligence, what are the practical possibilities for CAT in the real world?"

"Those have got to be aspirational goals," Negroponte, known for capturing the essence of a situation, answers. "The notion that you can have complete intelligence before you are forced to act is rare indeed. It's interesting to examine events after the fact to see the things you didn't know, or thought you knew. You hope that it's accurate even if limited in scope. The timely part is more important now than in Sun Tzu's day. In this day of information-technology you can integrate a lot more information than was imaginable in Sun Tzu's day."[23]

Gaddis once likened the distinctive contributions by GS scholars and practitioners to a well-written biography: it's "got to combine a sweeping narrative with very specific anecdotes," he explained. "If it's all narrative"—the professors—"then there are no human beings in it." But if all you do is war stories—the practitioners—"then maybe it's entertaining"—but not much else.[24] The added value of the practitioner is to connect the readings to the real world—what Negroponte calls "high-level facilitation."[25] Levin, Yale's former president, pointed out that most practitioners don't dwell on the broad historical context of their work or have the capacity to link it to scholarly thinking in history, the humanities, or the social sciences. But the good practitioners "have a really deep reflection on contemporary affairs and are very knowledgeable. The dialogue between the people who are very knowledgeable about the practical problems of the world with the people who have a broader conceptualization of history or politics or economics makes a powerful combination."[26]

Having so many instructors on hand makes the classes dynamic, with different professors and practitioners paired off to teach the seminars from year to year. When it came time to teach Machiavelli again, David Brooks took the lead, coteaching with Bryan Garsten from the political science and humanities departments. The material was the same. Borgia still has Romirro cut in half![27] But the emphasis had shifted slightly to include an exploration of Machiavelli as a moralistic thinker. "Machiavelli, who seems superficially immoral, is actually deeply moral," Brooks said. "He says, 'I love my country more than my soul.' That sounds a lot like anguish to me."[28] A week later Brooks wrote about the class in his *New York Times* column, relating it to President Obama's Machiavellian decision to use drones against terrorists. Even though they sometimes kill innocent children, they're more effective than any other "practical alternative," he writes. To Brooks, the president just hadn't taken his Machiavellianism far enough. He needed to recognize that "leaders are as venal . . . as anybody else." He urged Obama to appoint an independent judicial counsel to review the kill lists.[29]

This underscored one of GS's main points: Machiavelli isn't just dusty history. Like other classics, it's ahistorical — so relevant to contemporary US leadership and foreign policy that it's present on the editorial pages of the newspaper of record. And in another virtuous circle, the teacher is the same as the commentator, giving the Yale course even more street credibility.

The downside to having so many teachers in a classroom on any given Monday afternoon is the lack of airtime the practitioners generally receive. A one hour and fifty minute class can only tolerate so many interjections without detracting from what the full-time professors have to say. "One intervention each is just about right," said Negroponte, who added that he approaches the class as if it were an after-dinner conversation: "Here are some of the things I would have said about [my] view of the world."[30]

Solman often plays a role similar to the one he took in Hill's class on Machiavelli and Tooze's on totalitarian regimes. Adept at feigning outrage and asking well-placed follow-up questions, he goads professors and students to dig for answers. During Kennedy's seminar on the Romans, Solman asks him, "From the hindsight of history, surely we can tell why Rome fell."[31]

"No one reason," Kennedy answers, "which is not a cop-out. As Voltaire famously said, and American policymakers ought to think of this more seriously, 'If Rome and Carthage fell, which state can last forever?' Voltaire's answer: 'None.'"

During the Thucydides seminar, Gaddis tells the class that Pericles's decision to protect the Athenians by relocating them from the countryside inside the walled city presaged the Kennan strategy of distinguishing vital from peripheral interests during the Cold War.[32] "Pericles's strategy is rational," he says, "but people are irrational. People get very emotional when they see their crops being burned."

"What would you have done?" Solman asks him.

"That is a very good question, and I'm not sure I know the answer to it."

"But this is grand strategy!"

"Grand Strategy does not give you answers. What it does is to pose dilemmas."

Hill jumps in. "*Some* people's grand strategy does not give you answers."

Back in the Sun Tzu class it's Gaddis's turn: "If *The Art of War* is nonviolent, why does it start with executing concubines?"[33] The reference is to the king of Wu, a warlord who summons Sun Tzu and commands him to train 180 women from the palace into an orderly company. Sun Tzu divides the women into two groups, putting the warlord's two favorite concubines at the head of each column. Next he teaches the women a simple drill and orders them to perform it. But they burst into laughter. He tries again with the same result. Declaring that commanders are responsible for their troops' failure, Sun Tzu ignores the warlord's pleas and has the two concubines beheaded. The other women's laughter stops, and they perform the drill as he commands.

Saul, an undergrad, speaks up: "You don't always have to approach an incoming army head-on," he says. "A more effective strategy often relies on something more indirect. The point of beheading the concubines was to instill discipline on Sun Tzu's own army."

Gaddis: "Are you saying that to behead a couple of concubines points toward nonviolence, because it creates fear in the enemy?"

"Yes!" Saul replies, laughing uneasily.

"What is the benefit of winning without firing a shot?"

"You're not draining your country's resources."

Sun Tzu is famous for saying protracted operations are bad: any war that spans multiple harvests becomes counterproductive. Although he doesn't invoke the modern-day phrase "opportunity costs," he was the first known military theorist to talk about economics and damage to property. If you're rebuilding, you're not out planting or raising kids. You want to keep your population healthy, productive, and allied to you. It was at about this point during the Sun Tzu class a few years back that someone speculated on whether or not former secretary of state Colin Powell had read Sun Tzu. Negroponte, who was sitting along the wall, quietly emailed Powell, asking whether in his military training he had studied Sun Tzu. Powell emailed back promptly in an economy of words: "Sure. Economy of force." [34]

"In *The Art of War* there are no fixed rules," Negroponte now tells students.[35] "I think as we go on, and especially as we get to Clausewitz—maybe because I played a lot of poker as an undergrad at Yale—the closest analogy to war is gambling. It's important to be prepared, but there's no substitute for being in the arena. It's a different form of intelligence. It's the ability to think clearly in a difficult and dynamic situation."

"Is everything in this book [*The Art of War*] consistent with everything else in this book?" Gaddis asks, referring obliquely back to what Solman calls the course's "credo": the ability to hold two contradictory ideas in one's head at the same time.

"He lists qualities that are dangerous in generals," Annabelle, a Yale College junior, answers. "Compassion is considered a shortcoming."

"So what do you do when you get contradictory advice?"

"Intuition," Haywood says. "It may depend on whether you're a hedgehog or a fox."

"So how do you choose which you are?" Gaddis asks, homing in on the main point of the day.

"You're born that way," Haywood answers. "Tolstoy wanted to be a hedgehog, but he was a fox."

"How many people in this room have or have had coaches?" Gaddis asks. "Have they been consistent in the advice they gave you? How did you know what to do?"

"Based on prior experience," Haywood says. "You do what's best for your team. It's a combination of prior experience and in the heat of the moment you need to act."

"What do you do then? You can't wait for your coach to tell you."

"I go to prior experience. When you're forced to act your first tendency is to do what's in your own best interest and second is in your team's and in the split second you try to rectify them."

That's the answer Gaddis is looking for. "These things happen in sports and also in grand strategy," he says. "You have to size them up. What's the difference between wisdom and intuition? Wisdom has accumulated over a period of time. Intuition is the heat of the moment. The more wisdom you have, which is another way of saying 'more training,' which is another way of saying 'more experience,' the more wisely you'll make decisions in the heat of the moment. That's the premise of this course. This question is: "'When should you be a fox or a hedgehog? Can you be both? How do you know?'"

Act Two:
Summer Odyssey

With the lessons of Pericles, Lincoln, and other leaders still fresh, the next step is to use the theoretical training of the spring semester to make sense of the wider world. Both the GS summer and fall components are focused on the practical. But the work of the fall takes place in a classroom and involves assigned topics presented in teams. Then the students' task is to try to get a fingerhold on a nearly insoluble problem.

The summer project, on the other hand, is self-directed and personal—a rare, if not once in a lifetime, opportunity for GSers to do a deep dive into a strategic question of passionate interest. As one undergrad (GS '14) commented: "The privilege to design any summer experience is profound."[1] It's one of the few occasions in their academic careers when students craft and administer their own studies. Not even the sky would be the limit if they could figure out a strategic reason for exploring it and a way to get there at a reasonable cost.

The May-to-August interval rounds out students' careful reading of the great works, pushing them to go beyond the successes and failures of history and rise to real-world challenges: connecting limited means to ends, for example, and understanding firsthand what Clausewitz meant by "friction." An alumnus who taught in the Yale Young Global Scholars

Program, an adaptation of GS for high school students, said the summer component is "an example of what Professor Gaddis talks about with 'transferability.' It's not just studying the Cold War, but what lessons we can use now. It's meant to expand your horizons a little bit in terms of both time and space."[2]

Speaking to grand strategists at Duke in 2009, Gaddis amplified the reasoning behind the summer practicum: students, he said, "learn, from reading Clausewitz, that on battlefields 'the light of reason is refracted in a manner quite different from that which is normal in academic speculation.' Most of our students won't be on military battlefields, but their lives will be filled with other battles in which the light of reason will not be refracted as it was in our classroom. That's what we hope to give them."[3]

As with all things GS, the message is to think expansively. "I don't want to see any summer proposals like 'The Grand Strategy of How [the Connecticut town of] Branford Can Beat Off Condo Development,'" Kennedy told students during a Nuts and Bolts of Grand Strategy workshop held early in the spring semester. "That's not a grand strategy. Grand Strategy is about big things over time."[4] Gaddis made much the same point during orientation: "If you're curious about how Hannibal got those elephants across the Alps, this is your opportunity to find out," he suggested to the incoming GSers, adding, "I don't like the word 'internship.'"[5]

It's not that the professors are against students taking on summer work assignments. The pressure on professional-school students to burnish their credentials or nail down a job offer can make riding the rails in Siberia or examining colonial architecture in South America unfeasible. But even the most intellectually challenging internship, Gaddis was saying, is still circumscribed and, without the catalysts of surprise and/or struggle, unlikely to test GSers in ways that make the lessons of the great grand strategists their own.

Hill has a more pointed view. "We've created a generation of interns," he said over lunch one day. "They don't know that the intern culture has proliferated beyond all reason. Every college has created an internship for every student, and so it's become meaningless, but they don't know that."[6]

That's why the "odyssey," usually underwritten by the Brady-Johnson Program, is the preferred GS framework. It's not quite the arduous undertaking that Homer immortalized, but it's still a far-flung adventure that leaves room for serendipity. And if this requires speaking a foreign language, so much the better. One GSer traveled around India to study the Maoist insurgency, a journey he later described as more dangerous than his military tours of duty in Iraq and Kosovo; another packed off to Madrid, where, besides perfecting her Spanish, she learned how Philip II used music to build national character in the New World; a third, equipped with only intermediate Mandarin, penetrated parts of China that Westerners seldom see. There are stories of other students witnessing awe-inspiring sunrises, being trailed by wolves, and teaching Broadway show tunes to their "yurt-mates."[7]

Although the requirements are scant, the odyssey does have to be preapproved by the ISS assistant director. Jeremy Friedman explained that he based his decisions on "doability." "Did the student propose a project that he or she actually had the possibility to complete given his or her abilities, the methodology proposed, and the time and funds available?" This often meant helping shape both the conception and the logistics of projects and, on rare occasions, telling students that their proposals wouldn't work.[8] The other requirement, a five-thousand- to eight-thousand-word paper on what students learned about strategy, is due in the fall. But it's not the written assignment the professors are banking on to make the project worthwhile. It's the creativity and resourcefulness the GSers will have to use on the ground, an antidote to the mindless hoop jumping that higher education critic Deresiewicz[9] finds so common among, and damaging to, today's elite students. Conor Crawford, who spent his GS summer in 2011, between his junior and senior years, reporting on the grand strategy of Vatican II to update the Roman Catholic Church, said of his summer odyssey, "You're trying to paint a picture without knowing what it looks like. The students are asked not just to write about a grand strategy but to pursue a mini grand strategy of their own. You need common sense to get through it. You learn because you have to learn. I had to get interviews at the Vatican. How do you get church officials to talk to a college student? How do I get to the Vatican? How long do I prepare ahead of time?"[10]

For Crawford one incident stood out. "One night . . . I had a two-hour conversation in a monsignor's chambers, overlooking Saint Peter's Basilica in Vatican City," he said. "We sipped coffee and discussed all things Catholicism: from the finer underpinnings of our theology, to cosmology, to more traditional debates about the Church's place in modern society. It was one of the most impactful conversations on my life, and it would not have been possible without the summer grant from GS."[11]

Besides becoming fluent in Spanish, Matthew Blomerth (GS '08) said his summer project helped put him on his current career path, managing a team focusing on Latin America at a leading oil and gas market intelligence and research company. Blomerth traveled to Caracas to undertake research for a thesis entitled "Bolivarianism and Oil Boom in Venezuela," an analysis of the history of the oil and gas industry there, with a particular emphasis on how Hugo Chavez's government had radically altered the industry to make it the funding source for their broader socialist agenda. "This was a great experience," he wrote in an email, "not only because I got to do on-the-ground research but I also got exposed to the very intense political and security situation in Venezuela and truly understand many of the challenges, politics, and historical baggage of the country and many other parts of Latin America."

Blomerth continued: "Thankfully I did not get exposed to anything as bad as being chased by a drug cartel! Rather my experience was from living in a country where law and order had almost completely broken down. It was very risky to go anywhere after dark, and everyone avoided the police as they were considered to be just as dangerous as the criminals. Many of the people I interacted with had been victimized (i.e., home invasion, armed robbery, or kidnapping) . . . in the recent past. While I was very thankful to avoid anything happening to me personally, I gained experience from having to learn to adapt my travel patterns and way of life to a climate where the odds of something bad happening to you were rather high. It also helped me understand, culturally, the corrosive impact on a society when people live in a state of perpetual fear. It was also a highly instructive firsthand exposure to the endemic problems between upper and lower classes in some parts of Latin America. In Venezuela, the government's power largely derived from being able to channel the frustrations of the 'have nots' against the upper classes."

When Blomerth turned in his written assignment, he said, "Professor Hill was particularly interested in some of the fruits of my research that showed the financial channels allegedly being used by some officials in the Venezuelan government to use oil and gas revenue to support Cuba, which Chavez always considered to be the ideological model of a successful socialist state in Latin America. He passed it on to the State Department, because he thought I had found out some interesting information about how funds were being channeled internationally, and also because my interviews and research provided another perspective on government policies and actions being taken at that time."

He concluded: "Overall the experience really helped orient my career goals . . . having had the GS experience in Venezuela really provided a fantastic basis for my understanding of the region."[12]

Another alumnus, who asked not to be named, described the way in which his summer odyssey in Florence, Italy, helped hone his values. He was interested in studying the Palazzo Vecchio to see how it had evolved under different systems of government, from republic to oligarchy to autocracy. He found a place to live near the palazzo and the Uffizi gallery, where he visited the same paintings every day. "I don't know if I learned very much about power that summer," he wrote, "but I was face to face with concentrated beauty, which I think was much more important. Somehow that experience may translate into figuring out what your values are . . . Maybe by taking away the noise of the moment it forces you to measure yourself against the human version of eternity. As I continue to figure out how I think about the world, those are the experiences I keep returning to, the ones that help me remember what is important and what is less so."[13]

Daniel Khalessi (GS '14) spent the summer between two years of graduate school at the Jackson Institute studying ancient history firsthand. Starting out in Athens, he traveled through Greece, Turkey, Uzbekistan, Tajikistan, and India to retrace Alexander the Great's campaigns from 334 to 323 BCE.[14] On Alexander's journey, the conqueror slept with a dagger and a copy of *The Iliad*. Khalessi, traveling alone — sometimes on foot and often driving along mountainous cliffs on unpaved roads — left the dagger at home but brought his copy of Arrian's *Campaigns of Alexander* as "a field manual." No biography, however, could prepare him for the lessons he learned:

"The morning after I arrived in Athens I went to a museum and talked to an archeologist who said that Alexander hadn't left behind much of significance," Khalessi said. "When I asked why not, the archaeologist answered, 'We as Greeks are proud of our ideals — of Plato and Aristotle.' He showed me this plaque that Samos and Athens — the two city-states during the Peloponnesian War — had signed. It's one of the ancient treaties of statecraft. I realized I had to learn about what Alexander *didn't* do as opposed to what he did. At Yale there are a lot of ambitious people who have goals and want to do things. But our contributions are more important than our conquests."

Khalessi went on: "You can be a great commander, but if you don't have a broader purpose and understand your capabilities and limited means, then everything crumbles. That's exactly what happened [to Alexander]. After ten years it was over.

"In GS we study *The Art of War* and tactics and the genius of military commanders, but [the stop in Athens] made me realize that wars are metaphors for larger ideas. That lit a spark in my head. After Athens I went to the ruins of Troy . . . Alexander picked up the shield of his ancestor Achilles and took that all the way to India, but even that shield wasn't enough to protect him, because he didn't know when to stop. He conquered and had ambitions that were far behind his limitations. He didn't realize his limits. Most people I met, especially in Tajikistan, had never heard of Yale, but they knew who Alexander the Great was. But what is he remembered for? He conquered, but he didn't govern. He didn't leave institutions behind. Augustus knew when to stop expanding the empire and start building institutions. The modern legal system in the United States carries its essence from the Roman legal system. Our senate comes from the Romans. So he made a contribution that now lives on in the pillars of the United States."

Another lesson Khalessi learned was the "the balance between improvising and planning," he explained. "Sometimes you have to plan, but other times you have to throw out the plan and be brave." He'd wanted to fly from Tashkent, the capital of Uzbekistan, to Dushanbe, the capital of Tajikistan. Because of tensions between the countries, however, he had to cross the border on foot. Khalessi also had to improvise to communicate: "Before I went I had spoken to a number of Russian and Central Asian historians who told me I would have a language problem, because they only speak Russian and Uzbek. I started speaking Farsi, an unofficial language, and they started speaking it back to me. It's one of the things the Persians left behind there, and even though they were conquered twice, certain ideas outlasted the empires."

Khalessi continued: "I was afraid at the beginning of the trip. I was [traveling] alone for the first time and going to countries that people in the United States don't know much about, even people in high government positions. I went and gave myself to the people there and to their hospitality. They were some of the nicest people I ever met. In Tajikistan people invited me to their homes for dinner every night. By that time I had learned to accept risks and that if something happened I would deal with it. I did learn who to avoid and who not to. It's a question of being very friendly with people and interacting and not being afraid. This trip did teach me to conquer your fears. In order to conquer fear, you don't eliminate it, you balance it out with courage. If someone has no fear they're either lying or they're over-confident."

The trip changed him. "It made me want to make contributions in a more profound way. Before people used to ask, 'What do you want to do?' You name a position: secretary of state, or something — a name that boxes someone in. But this class represents an idea that cannot be boxed. That's what GS is. In other classes you learn details and issues, but this class [is about] ideas — balance, courage, limits — fundamental principles of living that are important in any job we do. These are the things you remember."[15]

While the summer experience is clearly transformative for many students, in hindsight other alumni regret not being bolder or more creative. Bryan Cory (GS '03), who took GS as an undergrad, said: "Wish I had made better use of my summer. I did a traditional internship in a very interesting and unique part of government, but I regret not spending it in Kazakhstan or wandering around China. That said my summer got me a security clearance that has served me very, very well."[16]

Campbell Schnebly-Swanson, who spent the first half of her GS summer working in an energy company in Houston and the second half living among fracking laborers at a trailer park in Cotulla, Texas, summed up the overall experience saying: "The summer odyssey is what you make it. Many people did little (essentially studying J. P. Morgan's or the UN's strategy while interning), but some people did amazing things and really took the opportunity to do something they would have never otherwise done at Yale. Again, it is what you make it, but for me, it was an unbelievable adventure."[17]

Speaking about the summer project at Duke, Gaddis said: "You'll return from this kind of internship with lessons that will stay with you for the rest of your life — even if you spend large portions of it stuck in some boring office working for some ogre-like boss. You'll have the inner confidence that comes from having done something extraordinary in your youth — from having gone through a school of surprise if not a school of danger — and you'll be able to draw on that experience in all the crises to come."[18]

The summer odyssey, in other words, is about stockpiling wisdom.

Act Three:
Fall Boot Camp

Poise Under Pressure

In the fall GS goes twenty-first century. The professors spend the first month of the semester looking at the current geopolitical environment under a broad theme such as "the new issues of grand strategy." In 2014 the first class discussion after the summer break considered Barack Obama's end of August press conference in which a reporter asked whether or not the president would consult Congress over possible US military action against ISIL in Syria.[1] Among other recent atrocities the extremist group had posted a video showing the beheading of American journalist James Foley. "I don't want to put the cart before the horse," Obama said. "We don't have a strategy yet."[2]

Meeting in the transept of Sterling Memorial Library, the students, a ragtag assemblage in flip-flops and shorts, are trying to get their heads back into big ideas. Gaddis, leading class, sits on the stage floor at the front of the room, his legs dangling casually over the edge. "This course operates on the presumption that having a grand strategy is a good thing," he says puckishly, amused at his inside joke. "I'm puzzled by the president's continued ability to say, 'We don't have a plan.' Often presidents say they have a plan when they don't . . . Is this brilliance and craft or incompetence and paralysis?"

Hill jumps in. "I think we're offtrack. We're drastically underestimating Obama. It's very clear that he has a grand strategy. If you think of us as being political counselors of a foreign country in Washington, assigned to analyze Obama, reading his speeches, etc." — as Hill once did; a Foreign Service officer living in Hong Kong, whose job was to analyze China — "it's obvious that Obama's grand strategy is one of pulling America out of a forward-leaning role. He feels America needs fundamental transformation."[3]

The last two-thirds of the semester are turned over, at least nominally, to the students, who undergo what's become a legendary GS initiation rite. Gaddis, Kennedy, Hill, and Co. have commandeered a military training exercise known as murder boards — practice briefs that officers give before they present the real deal to their higher-ups — for their own pedagogical purposes. The more commonly used, and genteel, name in GS is Marshall Briefs. It comes from an exchange George Kennan, hired as Secretary of State George Marshall's first director of policy planning, had with his new boss. When Kennan asked Marshall if he had any advice, the former World War II general's answer was terse: "Avoid trivia."[4]

But the exercise, under any name, is not genteel.

Working in teams of four or five, students craft two tightly written analyses of a single assigned topic delivered roughly a month apart, corresponding with a pair of Power-Point presentations given to their classmates and professors. It's only nominally the students' show, because as Victoria Hall-Palerm (GS '14) wrote in a *Yale Daily News* column about the experience, "From the very first sentences that come out of the presenters' mouths the professors" — who play the roles of cabinet secretaries, Joint Chiefs of Staff, and occasionally the president — "are at their throats."[5] One fall, during a briefing on the Arab Spring, GSers were surprised to face the real US Senator John McCain, who'd dropped by Yale on a Connecticut campaign swing. "We had some significant disagreements — very lively [conversation]," McCain told the *Yale Daily News,* "but that's what this environment's supposed to be all about."[6]

The topics are throat grabbing, too. Not just grand, they're galactic — contemporary questions, such as immigration, cyber-security, Ukraine and Russia, US policy on China, and America's global military responsibility that the country's political leaders grapple with but that most Americans are relieved they don't have to touch.

Africa: Take One

On the last Monday in September, two student groups are teed up to go first, taking their turns in the same decrepit classrooms where they unpacked the classics in the spring. In Room 217B, the Athenians are delivering a brief on fiscal solvency. Here, in Room 220B, a team of Spartans in sharp business attire standing nervously at the head of the seminar table, which takes up a good part of the room, have their PowerPoint slides ready for a brief on Africa.[7] Faculty members clustered at the table's far end (where the ceiling light is burned out) start things off.

John Gaddis: "I'm taking the liberty of designating myself National Security Adviser Susan Rice. Eric Li, who's joining us down here at the dark end of the table is the special assistant to China." Li, who runs a venture capital fund, was a guest that day.

David Brooks: "I'm Vice President Joe Biden."

John Negroponte: "I'm John Kerry, the secretary of state."

"It's a brave person who ate the first oyster," Gaddis/Rice says. "It's a brave team that dares to go first. You have not had the benefit of watching other flameouts, and we make special allowances in heaven for that."

With that it was the students' turn.

"I'm Leo Montay from the office of policy for the secretary of defense. This is Stan Reiker, Dane Smith, and Hamish Carr," says Montay, a midcareer, thirtysomething US Army major specializing in human intelligence, at Yale for his master's degree in African studies. "We'll be discussing current and future policies toward Africa. First: why Africa matters for US interests."

"John," Gaddis/Rice interrupts, turning to Negroponte/ Kerry, "in a real briefing would they call each other by their first or last name?"

"Either," Negroponte/Kerry says.

"In 2012 the United States published its 'U.S. Policy Toward Sub-Saharan Africa,' Montay says. "In 2014 the White House held its first ever US-Africa Leaders Summit."

"The US hosts leaders while China invests in Africa," Brooks/Biden says.

"Understanding Africa is important because of the

scale and nature of Africa," Montay continues. "It's the second-largest continent, and it's home to over a billion people. It has the second-largest population in the world. They speak more than two thousand languages. Islam is the largest religion, followed closely by Christianity. Africa includes fifty-four nations. It's the least developed continent and the most plagued by disease. But there's huge potential: there are rich mineral deposits, and it's the largest global market outside Asia."

Gaddis/Rice interrupts: "You're telling us some things we already know and some things that are completely implausible. Make sure your oral and written briefs connect."

"Could we experiment with the lights?" Gaddis/Rice asks, sounding petulant as he disrupts the presentation again.

"We ignore Africa at our peril," Montay says.

Smith says: "The US is failing, because we react crisis by crisis instead of having a grand strategy. Reacting has been a hallmark. We can't do it all. We have limited means. Avoiding terrorism and avoiding a large-scale war are vital interests. Promoting democracy is a desirable interest."

"Under what circumstances would a health epidemic represent a vital interest versus a desirable interest?" Boorman calls out.

"Are two categories enough: vital and desirable?" Gaddis/Rice asks, continuing the theme. "It sounds weird – odd to say that containing Ebola is desirable. You need 'prevent' as a third category besides vital and desirable."

Less than two weeks earlier, Obama had announced he was sending three thousand troops to build Ebola treatment centers in West Africa to help curb an epidemic that, as he said, was "spiraling out of control." In Dallas, on the same day as the GS briefing, Thomas Duncan, who'd traveled from Liberia, became the first person ever struck by Ebola on US soil, catapulting the highly contagious disease from a middling news item to a bold, above-the-fold headline—a place it would anchor for weeks.

"We're twenty-two minutes in, and we don't yet have a grand strategy for Africa," Brooks/Biden says. "You're giving foreplay a bad name!"

"Yes, sir!" Smith answers, as though snapping to attention. "We're talking about why the current White House strategy, which put priorities into four pillars—strengthen democratic institutions; spur economic growth, trade, and investment; advance peace and security; and promote opportunity and development—[should be rearranged]. We're talking about the same four pillars and reorganizing them to move security from last to first."

"What if vital countries are not willing to take responsibility for themselves?" Gaddis/Rice asks, immediately picking up on the selective engagement approach that the briefers invoke, albeit without labeling it—the idea that the US gets involved only in conflicts that threaten our long-range interests—that Montay would later describe in a phone call as a "nonstrategy strategy."[8]

"How does the strategy change?" Brooks/Biden jumps in. "I see a lot of moving around of boxes."

"We're proposing reordering the priorities," Montay explains.

"Usually when there's a change in strategy, something different happens," Brooks/Biden says.

"Why isn't this simply a rearrangement of the deck chairs on the *Titanic?*" Gaddis/Rice asks. "If our friend Henry Kissinger were here, he would say there's a rearrangement of deck chairs but no grand strategy. If world order is our priority, as articulated by Obama at the UN this week, why is it not more collaborative? And why is there no mention of the French? Keep it simple. Tell me: are these efforts a good thing or a bad thing? That's what I'm looking for in a grand strategic analysis."

Gaddis/Rice continues: "Mr. Carr, how would you define the term 'mercantilism'? It's a classic mercantilist argument. What Adam Smith says was outdated. Trade benefits all. Why is China's increasing dominance a threat? It goes against the US policy of free trade."

And then: "Let's get away from deck chairs and go to grand strategy for a moment."

"China is able to buy influence among African nations," Carr says. "What it comes down to, Madame Rice, is influence."

"You're saying it's okay for the US to increase its influence but not okay for China?" Gaddis/Rice asks.

"China can do whatever it likes," Carr answers.

"So you're saying we need to be more competitive with China?" Gaddis/Rice asks.

"Should we be promoting Subways or Bojangles?" Brooks/Biden asks. "Why should we use our shovels instead of Chinese shovels when there's only one world market to sell the diamonds or oil or manganese on?"

"It comes down to influence again," Carr says. "Our objectives are to increase market opportunities for US firms, improve the US commercial presence in Africa relative to China, expand the US political influence in Africa, and spur economic growth throughout Africa."

"If fighting a commercial war against China in Africa is your grand strategy," Li says, "the Chinese would be laughing. These things are so minor. The Chinese do have a grand strategy in Africa that is narrow and clear. One goal is to obtain access to natural resources. They are government owned. They operate like the East India Company."

Gaddis/Rice asks: "Given the American model of privately owned corporations, what can we do to offset China's state-owned model?"

"That's a great question, and I don't know that, sir, but I'll get back to you," Carr says.

"Don't say 'that's a great question,'" Gaddis/Rice says.

"I'm not ready to comment on that," Carr says, pivoting quickly.

"I urge the remaining briefers to do as the name implies," Gaddis/Rice says.

"Mr. Reiker, are you *reading* your brief?" Gaddis/Rice asks, feigning shock.

"No sir, I'm referencing it," says Reiker.

"Ebola has not come up," Gaddis/Rice says. "I've been curious to learn what the US should do. I had the feeling that in the written brief the couple of paragraphs [about Ebola] were tacked on."

"We crafted our strategy first," Reiker says.

"I'd like to see Ebola, which in many ways is an African crisis. This is what may have the potential to turn attention on Africa around. It may be both a crisis and an opportunity," Gaddis/Rice says, citing the frequent GS argument that in crisis there's opportunity.

"It's very challenging to come up with a grand strategy for a continent of fifty-four countries," Negroponte/Kerry says. "I would say 'health' [should be a priority] – not just Ebola, but the fight against HIV/AIDS is one of the things [of which] George W. Bush is most proud. I don't know about this China business – competing or keeping China out. I don't think we have the wherewithal to compete."

"As a grand strategy it's too diffuse," Li says. "You're getting confused about what American interests really are. When I go to a Chinese brief, it's clearer. You can touch it. One of the things I was surprised I didn't hear was about freedom of trade and piracy issues."

"When speaking in public, never waste a sentence," Brooks/Biden advises. "Your slides are too wordy. What is the defining thing right now? Rearranging the boxes has been the death of many Marshall Briefs over the years."

"I would lead off with the current issue leading the news right now, and that's Ebola," Gaddis/Rice says. "Secondary to that: peace and security and then economics. Since Professor Hill is not within earshot this afternoon, I'm going to bring up Kennan. The first policy planning staff came up with a grand strategy for a continent, and that continent was Europe . . . [Kennan's brief] said it's impossible to have a grand strategy for a continent, but we need to focus on a demonstration – a project that will have a profound impact. We focused on coal and steel production. The idea was to do it, because it's worth doing, not to contain the Russians. The thinking about China in Africa is a similar situation. [Your brief] is putting several carts before several horses. The project may be Ebola or HIV. This will have an impact all over Africa, even if aid doesn't flow all over Africa. That one document that Kennan and his staff of five created led to the Marshall Plan. The point is in a crisis Kennan rose to the occasion. Rearranging the deck chairs or boxes is for other people to do. The policy planning staff's job is grand strategy."[9]

Lessons Learned

The presenters aren't the policy planning staff; they're just four shellacked students in suits. But like the end-of-semester crisis simulation, the assignment involves a willing suspension of disbelief by professors and students. When his team prepared their brief on US policy in the Middle East, Justin Schuster (GS '14), a Middle Eastern and global affairs major, said that they became "so impassioned and engrossed, we were shirking all other work" in their non-GS classes. Finally an older member of their group, who worked for the Central Intelligence Agency (CIA), had to remind them that it was just an academic exercise. Schuster said. "I'm treating it like I'm briefing the president of the United States, which is really a testament to the professors. They're able to get the students to feel that way about the brief without being too overt."[10]

The pretense has its purposes. One is strictly practical. Those who complain that higher education doesn't prepare students for the real world could find little fault with the murder boards. GSers who go through them twice can't help but become better public speakers.

Schuster, who had to brief a US general for his global affairs senior project during the same semester as his Marshall Briefs, said he felt fortunate that the Pentagon briefing came last: "I was more nervous going before the GS firing squad than a decorated four-star general." The Marshall Briefs helped not only with briefing but also with "field[ing] unexpected questions from high-level brass," he added.[11]

The trial-by-fire training resonates with the majority of alumni. A student who emailed Gaddis and Hill after his graduation reported: "As one of my first official assignments in the Navy, my supervising lieutenant said, 'Ensign, please have a port brief on Mayport, Florida, to present to the wardroom tomorrow afternoon.'"

"Predictably," the alumnus wrote, "a 'port brief' isn't actually . . . defined . . . Mayport is a totally foreign place to me, and I knew this would be the first evaluation of my ability to stand up and present (in this case, pretty unimportant) information."

The assignment was both new and comfortably familiar. The email continued: "While it wasn't on the same intellectual or academic scale as a Marshall Brief, the port brief used the same skills I developed in GS, and it went well! So, thanks for the preparation and the once-frustratingly vague assignment—as you promised, that's what real life is like."[12]

As such experiences show, the Marshall Briefs offer GSers intangible lessons they'll need in leadership situations and in life. Many of these will sound familiar to readers of this book: learning to connect dots, make plans and be willing to toss them aside, tolerate uncertainty, and stand tough—traits and skills, or the lack thereof, of the leaders they studied in the spring. As one alumnus said, "The Marshall Briefs were the most educational part [of GS], for me, because they taught me the importance of both being deeply prepared but also being able to think on your feet (which is a practical application of the tenets we read in Sun Tzu and Thucydides)."[13]

How the professors teach the Marshall Briefs semester is inseparable from what they're hoping to convey. Gaddis, Kennedy, Hill don't subscribe to the every-kid-deserves-a-trophy approach prevalent today, or even a gratuitous pat on the back. This is boot camp—the intellectual equivalent of a midday twelve-mile, uphill run with a heavy backpack, blisters guaranteed. They're trying to teach if not poise, then what former ISS assistant director Bromund calls "marginal fumbling under pressure."[14] It's in this spirit that everything is fair game for their criticism: not just substance but the font they've chosen for the PowerPoint presentations and their general demeanor. (Note to future participants: the professors are above false praise, as in "That's a good question," but they appreciate the honesty of "I don't know the answer to that; I'll get back to you.")

Speaking to a group of visitors at Yale, Gaddis explained why the faculty is hypercritical during the briefs: "You need to build in certain levels of resiliency because you know that things will go wrong [in life]; you just don't know what. You need to build in backup systems or redundancies. About five years ago I had a student come to me in tears, saying you're trying to get us to fail. She was a tough student. She went off to join the marines. Yes, we are. That's what best prepares you to deal with unforeseen circumstances. You can learn to deal with these and not lose your cool, not lose your equanimity . . . The ability to deal with failure and to bounce back is one of the most important parts of the course."[15]

Solman told GSers during an end-of-semester wrap-up session on that year's murder boards: "What we're doing is overdoing it, because each of us only has one shot at you, and we're trying to be as useful as we can be in giving you the roughest time so you're tested in your presentation skills, your mastery of the material—a whole range of things for which this is supposed to be a crucible."[16]

At the same meeting, Hill said: "We are out of ourselves and into our role . . . so my constant attempt was to be a real asshole, because that's who you're going to meet when you're briefing the national security adviser."[17]

The majority of alumni agreed that the briefs' scorched-earth aspect is part of their value. Rebecca Yergin (GS '08), who took the class as an undergrad, said: "I view the Marshall Brief presentation as a memorable experience, even though at the time I found it very challenging. It is precisely this challenge that has made it stay in my head. I remember it as the only time in college where I worked very hard with a group to develop a plan and then had to answer very tough questions about it. It was really the only course in college that helped me appreciate how difficult leadership is."[18]

Matthew Tebbe (GS '04), who was enrolled in one of Yale's professional schools when he took GS, said: "My Marshall Brief team was the one singled out by Professors Hill and Gaddis as the 'absolute worst' one in the class. Professor Hill told anecdotes of his drafts being crumpled up and thrown back at him by Henry Kissinger and my team got that treatment during our presentation. All I remember afterwards was going to Anna Liffeys [a local Irish pub] with the team and having a drink."[19]

An alumnus who later worked in hedge funds, said, "I absolutely got torn to shreds by Prof. Hill during my Marshall Brief. It prepared me for the real world in that I often got screamed at by billionaires who were no more correct. Powerful people go berserk when the stakes are high enough (hundreds of millions of dollars in my experience) and are not always right . . . If you are going to take pain, it's better to do that in a classroom when serious money and human lives are not at stake."[20]

As brutal as the PowerPoint briefs can be, they're only the most visible part of the fall semester training — the culmination of weeks of debate, research, rehearsals, all-nighters, and more debate by students, many of whom have gotten through college having never worked on a team (but who, in the work world, will almost certainly find themselves sitting in an open floor plan with the rest of their "pod"). In the School of Public Health, where Bradley established her GS spinoff in 2010, a Yale organizational psychologist, David Berg, teaches a session to prepare students of different ages and with varying skill sets to work together effectively on their Marshall Briefs. "Today is about acknowledging that groups are complicated beasts," he said from a lectern. "The only time you bring people together with the same skill is when you need labor, like stuffing envelopes . . . We say we love diversity, but once we're together we wish everyone were the same."[21] Berg led a transformational exercise in which students experienced and then negotiated conflicts in individual and group identity, which proved fundamental to achieving a better group process.

Asked why the GS professors don't train their students on how to handle thorny group dynamics, Hill answered in an email: "[Psychologists have an] idea of how it should work, but no idea of what actually takes place in real life in high places, which can be vicious. So we do it the real life way. Visitors who know real life are impressed; educators and social science visitors are appalled by what we do. What we are trying to teach is how you make a team work when teamwork is impossible."[22]

Schuster said the experience helped him understand "what works and what doesn't" when you're trying to reach a consensus. "Strong minds and strong opinions led to Clausewitzian friction," he went on. "One of the best pieces of advice I've been given is you need to know when to talk and when to shut up, and that didn't resonate with our group. At the end of the day we realized that the most disastrous thing we could do was have dissent. You have to unify, because if there's dissent it undercuts the presentation."[23]

Another alumnus said, "The Marshall Briefs were the most rigorous thing I did at Yale. I'd never before been given so much freedom to do anything I wanted and never before been so vulnerable. It stress-tests your thinking, because you can't half-ass it. You learn group dynamics, you learn leadership, you learn how to think under pressure in a way that I don't think you're tested at Yale. There are exams, but you don't have people relying on you."[24]

The professors assign the same real-world conundrums that experts might spend decades trying to solve — and expect GSers to condense them into coherent two-hour presentations. It's the equivalent of the high school debate team arguing before the Supreme Court. Unsure how to approach something as unwieldy as US Middle East policy, the group discussed, and discarded, the idea of narrowing the focus, concentrating on US-Iran policy. When they tried to stay broad, they delivered what Hill described as a "*New York Times* policy brief" that, as Schuster put it, "viewed the region as a collection of individual, isolated, hot-button issues of the day rather than a web of interconnected challenges, shifting alliances, and complex power dynamics that reach across time and geography."[25]

The Africa group, which tried to sculpt an overarching policy for the world's second-largest continent, had trouble "figuring out what the issues were and how to package them," Montay said. "Carr believed this was an economic war with the Chinese, and we needed to get our licks in now. Reiker was strong willed about the environment. Smith was easy-going. I was just trying to make sense of the whole damn thing."

The group kept coming back to Ebola, unsure of whether to highlight or downplay it. "It was me who was most vocal, because I said, 'You can't have an Ebola strategy,'" Montay said. "That's not a grand strategy."[26]

Not only must presenters rise above the trees to see the forest, they also have to make sure that objectives laid out in the briefs fit true-to-life capabilities. This "happens much less than you would think," another alumnus explained. "Too often we set grand objectives without thinking how they will address those objectives."[27]

April Lawson (GS '08) said that her Marshall Brief on demographics was her "favorite academic experience at college in spite of the fact that we went first and had a terrible plan. We suggested that overall the United States benefitted from talent remaining in their home countries rather than [our] being a magnet for doctors and lawyers. I think it was ridiculous in retrospect and the professors made that very clear. It was really useful because it's very easy to say: it's terrible we have all this talent flowing from countries that need it to those that don't. But since every country has its own self-interests, can you actually apply that? The move from theoretical thinking to applied thinking was further and more difficult than people expected."[28]

Africa: Take Two

By the time Montay, Carr, Smith, and Reiker get together in Bass Library to decide how to approach their second Africa brief, the fear factor in the United States over Ebola has shot up dramatically. Thomas Duncan has died in Dallas; two of his nurses have contracted the virus, including one who's flown on a commercial airliner while ill; a doctor who'd treated Ebola in Guinea for Doctors Without Borders is isolated at a hospital in New York City, a day after he takes the subway from Harlem to a Brooklyn bowling alley; and President Obama has appointed an "Ebola czar" to calm panic-stricken Americans and close the gaps in protocol.

Gaddis, with whom Reiker had met after their flameout, suggests using Kennan's own policy brief on Europe as a framework for Ebola in Africa. "Everyone [on the team] liked this idea," Montay later recalled. "There was an element of simplicity in formulating a strategy around the gravity of Ebola. We were like, 'Hell, we tried it one way; let's try it another.'"[29]

A few days before Halloween the Africa team is back in the Hall of Graduate Studies for Take Two.[30] As is customary in GS, they will now be briefing different professors, which, as some of the students later said, added another layer of difficulty.

Charlie Hill is at the seminar table in the role of National Security Adviser Susan Rice, with Adam Tooze, acting as Barack Obama.

"You've asked us to consider the US grand strategy for Africa," Montay says, introducing the topic. "We've picked the Ebola crisis as a way to organize — "

"It's odd to pin an entire strategy for the US on what we hope will be a month or more of a disease," Hill/Rice interrupts.

"There have been ten-thousand-plus reported cases of Ebola in West Africa, of which some four thousand have died," Montay says. "In the US there have been a total of nine cases."

"I share my adviser's confusion of why we're starting with Ebola," Tooze/Obama says. "The numbers on the graph are strictly tactical. Why should I care more about this than AIDS deaths? If the numbers could run to a million, you've got my attention for the first time. If untreated . . . if we don't hit the 70 percent mark of containment — "

"It could lead to health, security, and economic crises," Smith says. "We're already seeing fear and political problems for the administration."

"More people will die of flu this season, right?" Tooze/ Obama asks.

"Yes," Smith answers, "but the fact remains that the fear is higher over Ebola than over flu. The existence of Ebola means it's a potential threat to anywhere in the world. There's a multiplier effect."

"You're saying someone is going to weaponize it?" Tooze/Obama asks, stretching Smith's point.

"I'm not in a position to say," Smith answers.

Montay says: "More people have died from Ebola in Liberia in the past year than of AIDS. We may be seeing up to ten thousand new cases every week by December. There are a number of political considerations in the US. [We may] be able to leverage US interests into a long-term strategy."

"[We propose] forming an Ebola task force (ETF) to report to the Ebola czar, who reports to the president," Carr says.

"What is the number of medical personnel necessary to contain Ebola?" Tooze/Obama asks.

"The UN has recommended seventy-five hundred. Right now the total number of people we've deployed is thirty-nine hundred soldiers and one hundred medical personnel," Carr says. "We have no frontline doctors. Cuba and Nigeria have doctors on the frontline. The doctor who went bowling in Brooklyn was working for a French agency."

"So the quantitative leap you're proposing is that we put thousands of medical workers in harm's way?" Tooze/ Obama asks. "Are we going to fly in thousands of doctors and nurses in the next couple of weeks?"

"We're recommending that you make a call for public service to put doctors and nurses on the frontline," Carr says. "That's what Cuba has done."

"Can I suggest that we strip out all these bullet points [on the slide]," Tooze/Obama says, "because you're suggesting that I make some Kennedy-like appeal to ask not what the medical profession can do for you but what you can do for the medical profession. Unprecedented."

"It's not incumbent on the US alone," Smith says. "We've mentioned Cuba. It's not fair to say the seven thousand people would be only Americans."

"Your slide is missing the point," Tooze/Obama says. "We need to be moving. There's urgency. What are the incentives? Are we going to conscript or send reservists?"

"Why this matters to US interests?" Reiker asks rhetorically. "Look at Walter Reed and his work with yellow fever. That allowed us to unblock the building of the Panama Canal."

"This needs to go via the military?" Tooze/Obama asks. "Should we be talking about the American Medical Association?"

"They're not military," Montay answers. "We're calling for a reserve corps. We would use the military for deployment from Fort Bliss and Fort Benning."

"Are you proposing to send six thousand?" Tooze/Obama asks. "We need to send three to four thousand to shame the rest of the world. Little known to most Americans, the Ready Reserve Corps are commissioned officers, so I'm their commander in chief. Can we even quarantine that number of people in the US?"

"We're trying to build the [facilities]," Smith says.

"Eighty percent of the US infected are surviving," Montay says. "Only 20 percent have died. We're hoping the vaccine will be ready by December."

"I'm taken aback by the scale," Tooze/Obama says. "It's not obvious from your brief that you're actually going to ask me to go out before Thanksgiving to ask three thousand Americans to do something that no one has been asked to do before. The casualty rates will be comparable to soldiers' in Iraq and Afghanistan."

"It's a legacy for you," Carr says.

"We see this as an opportunity for the US to take a leadership role," Montay says. "No one has the capacity to respond this quickly to the crisis. Our entry point is through Ebola right now."

"This is the most genuinely depressing brief," Tooze/Obama says. "It's a nightmare."

"You haven't given us the needs of the problem: care for the disease in West Africa; concerns about stopping travel. Then you could go through what are the Cubans doing; the World Health Organization," Hill/Rice says. "Maybe the Brits or the Japanese could do some of those things. This is all quick, get this stuff done by the US without any relationship to anyone else."

"As you mention, structures are important," Smith says. "Since we don't know the capacities of these other countries we thought it a weak brief just to call on them when you can call on them yourself, sir. We'd like to propose a medical NATO."

"We need to start with the need: what the disease is doing on the spot," Hill/Rice says, invoking the idea of a logic chain. "Then what is being done and by whom? And then, three, what the US can do and then A, B, C. Then in the future we can turn this into a medical NATO. Instead of just starting with medical NATO."

"I would like to roll you back," Tooze/Obama says. "Do you have a slide about the scale of these predictions? I'm haunted by the one million number. Unlike AIDS, where the logic of transmission is compelling, we should be able to interact with each other without transmitting Ebola. What do we know about social habits — are they getting that they have to change the way they live for the moment? Currently the infection rate is 1.7, which means that for every one person who has it, he gives it to 1.7 people where the transmission of AIDS is 1.1. How are these sites within these countries isolatable?"

"Mr. President, we don't really know," Montay says. "Now that it's gotten to urban centers, it's moving very quickly. We're focused on the urban centers, and we don't have a good understanding of what's out there."

"The CDC [Centers for Disease Control] has people on the ground to try to track the rural population that has been infected," Carr says.

"This is the first time this has moved to an urban center?" Tooze/Obama asks.

"It's always been in the countryside," Montay says.

"Once you get past critical thresholds in urban centers, we lose," Tooze/Obama says. "Where are the urban centers that we need to be focused on?"

"In terms of where things move in and out," Montay says, "there are two airports."

"This blows my mind," Tooze/Obama says. "It's a huge problem to Americans, but you're telling me it's in a country where there are only two airports? We can stop movement out of airports and seaports."

"It gets back to the fear of public health officials that it's going to start moving underground and then it will be harder to track," Carr says. "They need Excel spreadsheets. Public health officials say quarantine is not the right choice."

"Do they have a point at which quarantine becomes the right choice?" Tooze/Obama asks.

"As of right now there's not a threshold," Reiker answers.

Tooze presses the briefers on numbers. Finally, as the two-hour class is nearly up, Hill brings the presentation to a halt. "You can see that in the last twenty minutes you've really come alive," he says. "Your energy and ideas are really impressive, and everybody is involved. But there's no grand strategy. What stirs people up in our time are issues. Ebola is an issue. I say this in hopes that you take it away and think about it: it is no grand strategy. What you promised at the beginning of this brief never got off the ground. We interrupted you and threw you off. It's the intellectual time we're in, and it's been going on for a couple of decades at least. They teach issues at the Jackson Institute. Sometimes the issues hold together, and you have a conversation. What we've found year after year is that you go up to [grand strategy] and then you drop down to the issue. That level is what we're aiming at. And it hurts your head to think that. If you had stuck with the beginning of this it wouldn't have fallen into the fragmented sections until we hit on one that got everyone energized."

"I enjoyed this presentation, but probably for the wrong reasons," Tooze says. "This time I lured you into the trap that Charlie described through the force of the material. There were various missed opportunities to perform a jujitsu move to say, 'Sir, this is the grand perspective. If you let thousands of Africans die this is bad for Americans.'"

That evening Hill sent an email to Gaddis summing up his impressions: "an 'Africa' briefing today without Africa — all about Ebola, as led by Adam's pied piper-ing," he wrote. "I had to give my usual tiresome lecture, but nicely, at the end — the one about GS students seeking any excuse however implausible, to retreat to 'issues' in order to avoid GS thinking."[31]

Under the subject line "Flame-Out" he sent Gaddis a second email the next day in which he wrote: "Our session's problem was the 'issue' of Ebola, as I mentioned. When Adam juiced them up into full torque about the exquisite policy analyst details of the 'issue' with swarms of projected numbers dancing in their heads like sugarplums, the energy level in the room catapulted sky high; they loved it, not least because immersing themselves in the single issue relieved them from having to think Grand Strategically."[32]

It's Hill's familiar lament: that students start at the microlevel and never rise above it — a plane that never gains altitude.

The two professors arranged a December debrief to address this perennial problem.

Debrief

It seemed that the golden key would finally be handed out — that Gaddis and Hill would use the debriefing session to publicly debate their differing takes on grand strategy. But that's not what is happening here.

Instead Gaddis opens with a comment and a question. In past years, he says, "It was hard to tell whether the briefs got worse or better the second time around. It seemed to be a mixed bag . . . This year from my perspective it was a discernable improvement, sometimes even spectacular. The final briefs came close to being triumphant even . . . I would like to get some sense of why so that whatever we did differently this time we can make note to do next time."[33]

Smith speaks up: "We didn't know who we were going to brief the first time around. Given our experience we know what appeals to you as professors, and the second time it was easier to craft. There's a difference between heartbreaking genius and logic chains. We knew who to go to the second time around . . . I didn't know what success looked like for us to win, and I assumed I was going to lose no matter what I did. Maybe that points to a lack of moral fiber on my part."

Hall-Palerm had raised the same issue in her *Daily News* column: "Going into my first presentation, I had a deep-seated knowledge that there was a near-100 percent failure rate, if I was judging failure as anything short of my usual level of complacent preparedness," the piece states. "I knew [the professors] were going to ask me questions purposely to prove I didn't know the answer. I knew that if I gave an argument skewed to appeal to the more liberal of the professors, the conservatives would lash out, and if I tried to pander to the conservatives, the liberals would eviscerate me. If my team tried a conceptual framework, we'd be critiqued for ignoring specifics, and if we delineated concrete issues, we'd be docked points for losing sight of the bigger picture . . . With this project, there's almost no winning."[34]

The Africa team, which laid out a Kennanesque argument, with Ebola as the hook, at Gaddis's suggestion, is a good example. What seemed a sound idea to Gaddis, who spent seventeen years immersed in all things Kennan, didn't strike Hill or Tooze the same way—hardly surprising given that the professors also can't agree on the definition of grand strategy.

But where do the students fit in? And what does "winning" constitute?

On these questions, at least, the professors agree.

"What is the point of a brief in the first place?" Gaddis wonders aloud.[35] "One way is you're going to frame your brief in such a way that the policymaker will be happy and not lose sleep—what the policymaker wants to hear. Second is what the policymaker needs to know, which is not what they want to hear. It may keep them awake nights."

In a classic GS move he turns to a practitioner: "I want to throw this back to Ambassador Negroponte, who has done more briefings of presidents than others in this room. What is your objective when you go in? Is it your objective to tell that person what they need to know or to make that person happy and cheerful?"

"Clearly it's the former," Negroponte says. "Divide it into two categories. One is informational: an update on a particular situation. You're imparting useful up-to-date reliable information. The second, if it bears on policy, it's not going to be grand, but it will have grand elements of it. Try to reduce the issue to two or three essential elements that help your principle think more clearly about the issue. You've tried to improve the environment for intelligent thinking about an issue."

"I'm mystified by pleasing one professor or another," Brooks says. "If containment is our model of success, it's hard for me to believe that Kennan would have changed according to who he briefed. It seemed to me that all of the teams were good at amassing information. People were not good at how many slides to have—the technical aspects. The most difficult thing was to have an overarching concept. Whether in journalism or government that's the essential skill. It takes a willingness to go for a three-hour walk and think, 'What is my headline? What is my first sentence?'"

Gaddis says: "Victoria's op-ed made me think a lot about something we thought we were doing but were not. Most fundamental is to decide what *you* think as a briefing team. Your job is not to make us feel better. Your job is to master the topic and to decide what you think. I think the process of going through and getting contradictory information forces you to think critically. It seems to me that could be the most valuable aspect of this experience: that it sharpens your ability to decide what you think as an individual and team."[36]

It comes back to the central point of GS—the idea that decisions have to be made before all of the facts are in.

Act Four:
Winter Leadership

Today the process to elect a new US president has stretched to twenty-one months. But in the GS crisis simulation the electoral season lasts about twenty-one minutes. Presidential and vice presidential candidates deliver a stump speech. Ballots are cast. The winners are declared. Then, on the first Saturday in December, it's over to the second floor of Linsly Chittenden Hall, where the classrooms become West Wing offices and Senate hearing rooms, the building's leaded windows and oak wainscoting standing in for the grandeur of the White House and US Capitol. In 2014 the Oval Office is occupied by Laura Wheatley, a senior ethics, politics, and economics major (EP&E) in Yale College, and her vice president, Raquel Silver, also majoring in EP&E. The president appoints a scaled-down cabinet and a few key ambassadors, while the other GSers assume the roles of congressional members or bloggers, who work for three fictional media outlets of different political persuasions, Justice Now, Freedom Now, and Foxes & Hedgehogs. Belying its name, which conjures an image of NASA during an Apollo launch, the control room is resolutely low tech. It's made up of a revolving set of professors, ISS administrators, grad students, and military personnel whom Gaddis calls "the reality check," and guided by Hill's stack of handwritten cards, each spelling out a different disaster. Hill riffles through the cards, many of which he comes up with as the simulation progresses, and hands his selection to Gaddis. If approved, the card is passed down the table to an information technology assistant, who types it into a Google Doc where the dispatch is distributed to GSers in real time under the disclaimer "This document has not been approved or endorsed by the Federal Government, the State of Connecticut, or Yale University, and it has not been produced by an agency of the Federal Government. It is a simulation, prepared for educational purposes only." In yet another blending of fact and fiction, the dispatches in the Google Doc often appear under the names of real news organizations, such as NPR or the *Wall Street Journal*. No wonder Hill told the students in a presimulation briefing, "I would underline that information is the name of the game. You've got to have an information central that is taking in everything so that some one or two of you has information under control at all times. You can't have it coming in piecemeal and someone saying that's not important and putting it away."[1]

The crisis simulation stands in for the program's final exam, testing GSers' ability to handle international and national crises sensibly and to make tough decisions in a compressed time frame. Following the Marshall Brief, the objective is to manage under pressure in a situation that makes the students draw on all of the principles and skills they've learned over the past year. But it's not just a rehash. Shuttling between meetings held in hallways and classrooms and via cell phone, the president and her advisers are under pressure to learn and adapt until the curtain falls late in the afternoon on the second day. One idea they don't necessarily grasp beforehand, as Jeremy Friedman later explained, is "that international diplomacy . . . is not simply a matter of explaining your views until the other side agrees and you can hammer out a deal. Students often seem to think that international relations is like business in which everyone wants to make money, and you just have to find a deal where both sides profit. But the thinking of foreign governments and leaders is often opaque, they may have entirely different interests or understandings of a given situation, and they might not want to reach a deal – they might want to stall, or intimidate, or undermine, etc., and that might be the extent of their policy. Or they might not even have a policy."[2]

The backbone of the exercise is the National Security Strategy (NSS), a takeoff on the legislatively mandated statement the real president submits to Congress to communicate the administration's strategic vision. The GS professors expect a document that integrates the thinking behind the semester's various Marshall Briefs. "We believe you have accumulated wisdom and implicitly you've been thinking about the connections," Gaddis says in the final session of the semester, leading up to the crisis simulation. "How does Africa relate to China? How does immigration relate to economic conditions? This is the opportunity to pull them together."[3] Wheatley puts the NSS in simpler terms: "what [the United States] should do in hot spots and on hot topics."[4]

Besides providing an intellectual framework for decisions the president and cabinet make during the simulation, the

NSS acts as an organizing element for the first Saturday. It must be completed and adapted into a speech that the president delivers at 4:00 p.m. in the same makeshift GS briefing room where mock press conferences and bill signings usually take place.

The deadline is firm. But like the real White House, there are plenty of countervailing forces that can push the schedule, and the actors, off course. "The world will not stand still while you are preparing your national strategy statement," Gaddis cautions. "You can assume foreign policy will have to be conducted, domestic issues will have to be addressed, cabinet members will be attending to their own responsibilities, diplomacy could be carried on in English or also in difficult foreign languages so you should be prepared for that as well."[5]

The crisis simulation parallels Washington's current political environment, which means that Wheatley's presidency, like Barack Obama's, is a Democratic administration under pressure to burnish its legacy in the aftermath of calamitous midterm elections. First on Congress's schedule is to take up Wheatley's nomination for defense secretary to replace Chuck Hagel, who resigned in the fall. But Congress is also free to schedule its own hearings, just as, down the hall, the White House press corps' job is to follow unfolding events and stir up political mischief (inventing personal scandals isn't allowed). "Keep in mind the current climate in which anything you say can be blown up out of proportion most unfairly and most unjustly, but nevertheless that's how it happens," Gaddis tells GSers in a day of orientation he gives every year.[6]

The biggest threat is the control room. The professors and staff intersperse the hours leading up to the speech with ceremonial duties: among other events Wheatley has to make time for a photo-op with the 2014 World Series Champion San Francisco Giants, deliver a speech commemorating the 130th anniversary of the Washington Monument, and host Seychelles president James Michel at a bilateral meeting in the Oval Office. "It's a publicly released schedule so if you depart from it, people will wonder what crisis is afloat," Gaddis explains. The professors also sift through Hill's cards, dropping grenades small and large into the day. "You can think of it as God making problems," Gaddis tells GSers.[7]

Each morning throughout Wheatley's term the control room sends her a president's daily brief, a combination of real and fictitious news stories to advance the story lines introduced during day one of the crisis simulation and to set new scenarios in motion for day two. Each item presages a potential international or domestic disaster—catastrophes brought about by weather, the economy, sensitive international relationships, and mistakes made by the president and her advisers.

By the end of day two, at least one of these situations—or a new one—will mushroom into a full-out crisis that will demand Wheatley and her cabinet to act decisively, applying some of the principles articulated in the NSS the prior week. They have to work to gauge which one it will be, something not even the control room knows going in. Besides "what?" the question that hangs over the day is "how?" Will the presidential team deal with the crisis coolly? Will their actions be consistent with the president's grand strategy? Or will the previously stated principles collapse as they try to contain the conflict? And, finally, can they limit the damage, or does the world blow up?

Some observers are convinced that the simulation exercise is more entertaining for the professors than it is instructive for students. The benefits to GSers do prove somewhat uneven: those assigned to be members of Congress and bloggers are usually on the periphery of crises and have to invent work. But for others the experience is irreplaceable. Amira Valliani (GS '09), who took the course as an undergraduate and worked at the White House National Security Council and as a special assistant in the Office of the Secretary at the State Department before enrolling in a joint MPA and MBA at Harvard's Kennedy School and Wharton, commented that she "still remember[s] the crisis simulation as [one of] the most valuable academic experiences of my Yale career."[8]

As GSers arrive at Linsly-Chittenden Hall the first morning they learn that, overnight, during an Umbrella Movement protest in Hong Kong, an American, Cicero Lock, was taken into Chinese custody in an undisclosed location, and an American shoulder-launched missile downed an Iranian air force fighter-bomber conducting airstrikes against ISIL positions in Iraq.[9] Grim financial news pouring out of Ukraine and Georgia has the day's *Wall Street Journal* calling for a "bail in" of private creditors in Ukraine, and *New York Times* columnists are urging a Marshall Plan for the Black Sea. An early-morning oil spill in Bismarck, North Dakota, outrages congressional Republicans, who blame the accident on Wheatley's refusal to approve the Keystone XL pipeline. The president's press secretary, Arthur Knoop stirs an international firestorm by uttering an expletive in a press conference.

That's just in the first hour.

Keystone, the 1,179-mile pipeline that would transport about eight hundred thousand barrels of petroleum per day from Alberta, Canada, to the Gulf Coast, immediately becomes a contentious issue between Wheatley and congressional Republicans. Talking with cabinet members about the administration's official stance, the president says, "I want it to be generally negative."

"According to the American Petroleum Institute there are more spills from pipelines than trucks, with trains third," an adviser says. "Should we put that on the White House website?"

"It's better to come from American Petroleum Institute," the energy secretary says.

Although Leo Montay is confirmed as the new secretary of defense, Minority Leader Jack Farahany schedules a press conference to draw attention to what he calls Montay's "inadequacies." Grasping the political truism that it's bad to waste an audience, Farahany uses the forum to pressure the Wheatley administration on Keystone. "The Keystone pipeline should have been passed by now," he tells the White House press corps, and announces a new social media campaign on Twitter, "#BuildthePipe," to stir public opinion in its favor.

At White House press secretary Knoop's midmorning briefing, he's asked if there are any changes in the president's thinking on Keystone. "We believe that oil security is extremely important," Knoop says. "We do not feel the Keystone pipeline is the answer. Spills from pipelines are much more frequent than spills from trucks. They pose a security risk. There are miles of unguarded pipeline."

A reporter from the *Dallas Morning News* raises his hand. "Keystone will create sixty-five thousand more new American jobs," he says.

Energy Secretary Rick Fine answers: "The Keystone Pipeline will create fifty permanent jobs."

Reporter: "That's a huge discrepancy! Two-thirds of the American public is in favor of the pipeline."

But this is only one issue on the president's plate.

The wires are also reporting an explosion at a medical marijuana dispensary on the University of Colorado campus, with a death toll so far of fifteen. The Mexican Sinaloa drug cartel, whose profits have plummeted since the legalization of marijuana in several American states, claims responsibility.

Another drumbeat with which the White House must contend is the authorization for the use of force resolution against ISIL (in real life the issue was bogged down in political gamesmanship, with Obama saying he would seek congressional authorization for the US-led military operation already under way but had the authority under a resolution passed by Congress in 2001). NPR reports: "Conservative members of Congress are beginning to wonder publicly about why Minority Leader Farahany hasn't taken the lead in shaping a new 'authorization for the use of force' resolution. Inaction by Wheatley is beginning to raise constitutional questions about White House intentions and competence."

When there's no reaction on either side, a *New York Times*

editorial gooses the issue: "The Wheatley administration's studied avoidance of the need for a renewed 'authorization for the use of force' against ISIS in the Middle East, and the opposition party's failure to come up with a coherent position on the issue has brought the nation to a constitutional breakpoint. If President Wheatley does not speak to this pressing issue in her speech today on the National Security Strategy, it will undermine all else she says about US security policy—and raise doubts about her presidency overall."

More than ginning up disasters from scratch, however, the control room prefers to exploit students' blunders that they then stretch to the bounds of realism. Press spokesman Knoop's "aw crap" faux pas is one example, and the decision by Wheatley's Homeland Security Department secretary to call the Coast Guard to clean up the Bismarck oil spill in the Missouri River instead of the Army Corps of Engineers, which has jurisdiction, is another. Wheatley also accepted a request from Liu Yongqing, the wife of former Chinese president Hu Jintao, for a White House meet and greet. Hanging up the phone after a conversation in Chinese about the faux pas, Friedman, who's fluent in Chinese and Russian and was playing the role of a Chinese diplomat, told the control room disdainfully: "The first [student] didn't speak Chinese. It might have some negative impact on Chinese-American relations. I asked what they'd think if we invited George W. Bush to come to Beijing."

But the biggest Wheatley administration mistake, and the most perplexing, is the stream of communiqués that come into the control room revealing covert actions. When the professors and staff receive the first classified message,

Gaddis asks, "Why are they telling us? I think we should put this out as a leak. Go verbatim with that. Then we can have an investigation. This can be a breaking news story on CNN. I want this to go out very quickly."

Soon the *Huffington Post* reports: "Sources in the American intelligence community have leaked an intra-governmental message of the Wheatley administration: The CIA, which has sources within the 'Umbrella movement,' has decided to provide the standard set of incentives to the students in Hong Kong to continue their movement. This is covert support and [has] no official US government stamp on it."

The leaks keep coming, and the control room keeps publishing them. From the *Guardian*: "Leak from an internal US government source: On 6 December 2014, Commander, Joint Chiefs of Staff (C/JCS) held a secret meeting with senior Iranian defense officials in downtown New Haven. The discussion focused on Iranian/US coordination against ISIS targets."

On Fox News: "Bizarre, Puzzling, Dangerous Leaks Keep Flowing Out of the Wheatley Administration": "Highly classified US-Australian contacts on naval operations in the Western Pacific emerged today in the press, the latest in a recent stream of secrets indicating that either the Wheatley administration is riddled with incompetent personnel or that a Snowden-like 'mole' is at work and play in Washington."

Gaddis tells his control room colleagues, "Former students in the past hacked in from Washington, but that's not what this looks like. I don't know if [the Wheatley administration] thinks they have to include this information with us. The control group is not privy to their internal communication."

Hill says, "They're departing from the current [Obama] administration, where they just take executive action and don't consult. Whatever it is, it's a caution against sharing information casually."

As the information continues to come in, the ramifications grow: "Canberra: Sources inside the Australian government indicate that it has cut off intelligence cooperation with the American government due to the recent preponderance of damaging leaks."

"After the *Guardian* disclosed the existence of secret US-Iran talks on targeting ISIS in Iraq today, senior officials in Saudi Arabia expressed dismay and anger over the perceived American betrayal. While it has been widely assumed that US and Iranian forces were quietly deconflicting operations within Iraq for some time, the revelation of direct, high-level discussions in Washington marks a major uptick in bilateral cooperation. 'Washington needs to remember who its allies really are,' an unnamed senior Saudi official told the *Times*. 'We will not stand idly by as Iran is handed the keys to the Middle East.' Meanwhile, the Iranian Government was quick to disavow any cooperation with the United States. Ayatollah Khamenei, in his weekly address, stridently condemned the 'Great Satan' and reiterated that the United States remains the greatest threat to regional security. Iranian press reported that several Iranian defense officials may be relieved of duty as a result of the scandal."

Later, during a press briefing, Gaddis, in the guise of a

White House reporter, asks Press Secretary Knoop, "Is the administration going to reshuffle to deal with the sudden flood of sensitive leaks that have appeared? It has puzzled our allies at home and abroad. What is the administration going to do? Is it stupidity or treason? Do you have any accounting of how security has broken down?"

Despite their blunders the students seem to fully occupy their roles, even when no one from the control room is watching. At noon, when Wheatley walks out to the Nathan Hale statue on Old Campus, a stand-in for the Washington Monument, where she delivers a speech in a cold drizzle, another student, pretending to be a US Marine officer, holds an umbrella over her head, as real-life protocol would dictate. As Wheatley said later, the military called me 'm'am,' which made me stay in character."[10]

In the afternoon the president meets with Congress in a round robin to get their input on the NSS. "The perception from our end is that the US has retreated from its role in the world," Republican Speaker Farahany says. "We want a strategy that reasserts America's role in the world. The [other] thing is natural resources and the role of oil. The *key* thing we're looking to see in the NSS is the Keystone pipeline. There has been foot dragging by the administration. It would be a tremendous sign of cooperation. If you work with us on this it opens a number of other things the administration wants to do."

Wheatley answers: "I don't envision us changing our stance at this time, but I'm open to including something in the NSS about how we're open to reviewing that option. I encourage you to find [the EPA administrator] and [the energy secretary] and say the president is open to saying something about the Keystone pipeline."

The administration is also making efforts to be proactive, flooding the control room with requests for meetings, which has the professors and staff trooping to different Linsly-Chittenden Hall classrooms and hallways in the role of one ambassador or another. But GSers' efforts can sometimes fall flat. Gaddis reads one administration request for information aloud: "'What is the American Navel presence in Asia right now? What is the American Navel presence in the Middle East right now?' It's spelled 'navel,' so we can say, 'No information whatsoever on navels.'"

At a meeting of senior staff in the domestic policy room, one adviser says, "Let's just start doing stuff. Let's decriminalize marijuana." Indeed, a few hours later, Attorney General Justine Harlin announces a bipartisan bill that legalizes marijuana and aims to fix the US justice system, which suffers from "structural racism and pervasive mistrust among the American people."

The control room doesn't want to give up on Keystone XL. After zero administration progress has been made it stages a bigger spill crisis, this time near Washington, DC: "Amtrak's Northwest Regional 1494 Boston to Richmond passenger train was knocked off the rails outside Wilmington, Delaware, when an 85–tank car train carrying liquid shale oil from North Dakota to a refinery on the Delaware River itself derailed with one tank car smashing into the middle of No. 1494," the wire report on the Google Doc reads. "No deaths are yet reported, but scores are injured and polluting oils have run into nearby waters and halted all East Coast rail traffic."

The *Wall Street Journal* follows the accident with an online editorial under the headline "Wheatley's Utopian Energy Policy Puts Environment, American Lives at Risk": "With her single-minded focus on a utopian ideal of a carbon-free future, she has ignored the very real and immediate costs to the environment, to the broader economy, and to public safety," the post reads. "Denying permits for oil pipelines such as Keystone XL does not lessen the demand for this oil. Rather, it merely shifts the burden of oil transport onto American roads and railways. Not only are these means vastly less efficient — and, incidentally, require burning a lot of diesel fuel — they also sharply increase the potential for accidents, as the Dakota truck spill has illustrated all too clearly. As bad as this derailment is, one could easily envision a much worse catastrophe if it had occurred in a populated area — or on a track shared by one of the passenger trains of which Democrats are so fond."

Within minutes Wheatley caves. She signs a Keystone bill into law that includes a carbon tax and bolsters the economy by earmarking half of the pipeline revenue for middle-class tax rebates. "The reason why we thought this was good to move forward is that this administration doesn't want climate change to destabilize," the EPA administrator says at a hastily called press conference. "Oil spills are dangerous and toxic when not managed in the right way. We've taken extra precautions to make sure the pipeline is sealed."

As secretary of state under Ronald Reagan, George Shultz understood the difficulty of keeping the broader picture in mind amid the turmoil of everyday governing, an observation not dissimilar from Kissinger's that "the convictions that leaders have formed before reaching high office are the intellectual capital they will consume as long as they continue in office."[11] Twice a week, therefore, Shultz would hold all calls except from his wife and the president, move over to a comfortable chair, and sit for forty-five minutes with pad and pen. "I would take a deep breath, and say to myself, 'What am I doing here? What are the broad objectives? What are we trying to achieve?'" he said in a phone interview. "So if we had a strategy you're . . . refreshing yourself on it all the time."[12]

Wheatley can't do the same in the compact time frame of the crisis simulation. But even as she nears the deadline for her four o'clock speech, she seems unfazed by the day's distractions and disasters.[13] An effective delegator, she leaves the task of drafting the NSS and the presidential address to her chief speechwriter and other advisers. Looking back on the crisis simulation a few weeks later, she explained, "I was trying to avoid the cult of personality" and "I trusted my team. I knew [the vice president] and [national security adviser] were there. They all care about A's as much as I do."[14] And so at four fifteen that afternoon, preceded by "Hail to the Chief," President Wheatley takes the podium in the briefing room to address an exhausted White House press corps, who've kept up the charade since breakfast seven hours earlier.[15] "My fellow Americans," she begins. "Tonight, I want to speak to you about the state of the world today, and to outline our strategy to strengthen America's leadership, to safeguard America's interests, and to ensure America's security."

She continues, hitting all the trouble spots: "America and her allies find the world at a crossroads. In the Middle East, terrorist organizations like ISIL have continued to destabilize the region, establishing laws and policies based on radical religious ideology and committing acts of pure evil against innocent civilians, including Americans. In Russia, President Vladimir Putin's government has ignored numerous warnings from the international community and continued to violate international law with its actions in Eastern Ukraine. Russia's reckless actions are a threat to the world, and its defiance in the face of international condemnation is hardly the behavior of a world power committed to peace and democracy. In Western Africa, thousands of men, women, and children continue to endure the ravages of the worst Ebola outbreak in history. And in China, leaders have focused on building isolated, independent institutions rather than engaging constructively with the international community.

"We must also recognize emerging threats: the real and immediate threat of climate change," she says.

"To confront these challenges, America needs a comprehensive approach focused on strengthening our partners, prioritizing our resources, and providing the world with strong and steady leadership. Most important, the United States cannot do this alone. That's why the heart of our strategy is the idea the we are *stronger together*."

The speech is filled with the patriotic jargon one would expect under the circumstances. But it was delivered with a poise that few college seniors could muster.

Later, explaining the genesis of her NSS, Wheatley said she'd talked with some of the professors before the crisis simulation began about Obama's strategy: "Professor Hill said that President Obama's grand strategy is withdrawal. I tried to find a way to say that the president — myself — seeks two things: a return to life, liberty, and the pursuit of happiness, which means let's look inward and let's not take on so much. Some of that got too boiled down in the original NSS. [My points] weren't as well communicated as they could have been. Since I was running back and forth, I put [the document] in [my classmates'] hands. I would have expressed it differently — perhaps more bluntly. I would have said those two aspects more directly and tried to weave them through. We wrote the document there so we found ourselves where it was challenging enough to get people to finish their part without saying you have to weave these themes through. That would have been a lot to expect."[16]

Maintaining the pretense throughout the next week, the professors send Wheatley a "Strutmore analysis" of her NSS, in the style of the real-life online Stratfor. "What's missing within the pillars are prepositions," the memorandum reads. "Adapting global order to what in the 21st century? Establishing the U.S. as a visionary *for* what? Recognizing priorities *as* what? Instead what we get is repetitive rhetoric about the existence of challenges and the need for cooperation. Together with, on p. 13, an incomplete paragraph inviting readers to fill in whatever they like."[17]

Asked for his assessment of the GSers' performance, Hill emails: "What we did on Saturday generally was pre-actionable, as in the Cicero Lock case; there was little they could do until we decided to take it further, which we may, or may not do on this coming Saturday . . . All the while, they were doing as you say, putting forward their own initiatives, which we stymied, such as their telephone call initiative to Palestinian President Mahmoud Abbas (me), which he swatted away easily and they dropped. By the end of the day their agenda of initiatives looked pretty ragged."

He concludes: "But the serious stuff will start Saturday. I wish I knew what it's going to be."[18]

It's the second Saturday.[19]

President Wheatley has just returned to the situation room after presiding over a 3:30 p.m. Hanukkah menorah lighting ceremony on the White House ellipse. Before she was called away she was in the midst of discussing a portentous situation with her international advisers and intelligence team. It seemed that Iran and Israel were on course for a potential nuclear showdown, and the group was calculating how many troops could be moved into the region, and from which locations, in case they had to put that contingency into play quickly. But a lot can change in fifteen minutes. Now an ominous dispatch about a different but equally grave set of events, this one involving Russia, has come in:

VILNIUS

An armored column made up of at least ten Russian T-72/S main battle tanks crossed the border from Belarus into Lithuania early this morning, apparently on a route that would lead them into Kaliningrad — a geographically noncontiguous part of Russia proper. The column has taken no action regarding Lithuanian territory or population, confining itself to transiting this Baltic nation. Russian troops have been stationed in Belarus at least since 1995.

Within minutes, another dispatch amplifies the first:

The Kremlin announces "The Putin Doctrine": all parts of the Russian Motherland must be connected, not by concession or understanding, but by geographic land corridors that will be legally part of the sacred territory of Russia. This in the current instance involves the corridor from Russia to Kaliningrad and the corridor of Eastern-Ukraine to Crimea. All nations must respect The Putin Doctrine.

"This Putin doctrine has no time limit on it or no legal backing, so this is not necessarily a crisis," Wheatley says, after her briefing. "It could be nothing but rhetoric."

"It's implicitly saying, 'We want to annex these regions,' UN Ambassador Tanya Ellerbee volunteers, "but we can't jump to that."

Trying to measure the situation's seriousness and hoping for the best, Secretary of State Dustin Lash places a call to the Lithuanian minister. But the news only gets worse. "We're in great need of your military support," the minister says. "The situation at present is that the Russian armored columns have crossed our territory into Kaliningrad, and yet the armored column is leaving behind forces that are holding the corridor. It is not a transitory operation but apparently an occupation along a corridor that appears now to be taken and occupied by the military forces of Russia."

"Have you been in contact with Russia?" Lash asks.

"We've tried, but our communication has been rebuffed," the minister says. "This is a moment of extreme historic significance, not just for my country. I have to ask your support for putting Article V of the NATO charter into effect."

Hanging up, Lash relates the conversation to the president: "There are two takeaways," he says. "It's a permanent presence, and he wants to invoke NATO Article V."

"They don't have enough troops to take control," Ike Valenti, the US ambassador to Russia, says of the Russians. "They have a domestic problem."

"The question is whether or not we want to engage in an act of war," the press spokesman, Arthur Knoop, says. "I don't think they think we have the balls to attack militarily."

"Why are you so rapid to call this an attack?" Valenti asks Knoop.

"Because the Lithuanians are calling this an attack," Knoop shouts, amping up the discussion.

"Our job is to work with the Lithuanians to back down the rhetoric," Valenti responds calmly. "If it's an attack, and we call it an attack under Article V, we have to go in. We need to work with the Lithuanians and the Russians so that this does not mean we lose one-third of Lithuania."

"Good effing luck," Knoop says bitingly. "Move assets into the region. We need to create a contingency plan that's military, because I think that's where we're going."

"I'm on board with moving assets into the region," Hamish Carr, the director of national intelligence says.

"We already have the NATO special response team after Crimea," Valenti says. "What worries me isn't the tanks on the ground, it's what we don't see—the agitation behind the scenes."

"I don't care about that right now," Knoop says. "I care about the general stability of NATO. We have to deal with the immediate problem at hand. We have to deal with tanks and troops."

"I disagree with your premise," Valenti tells him.

"Even if you disagree with the premise," Carr interjects, "the resolution is not that far apart."

"The British have a carrier, and the French have a carrier," Knoop says, turning to Wheatley.

"Reach out to the French and British and find out where their carriers are," Wheatley says.

While they're deliberating, Congress votes to declare war on Russia.

"How does this end?" Valenti asks the group assembled in the situation room.

"In light of the stronger together doctrine we want assurances that NATO will assist us in defending Lithuania," Wheatley says. "This is not an attack on Russia. It's a defensive effort."

"We object to Russia's violation of Lithuania's [sovereignty]," Knoop says. "They have their right to Kaliningrad, but they don't need a corridor. They can simply ask Belarus and Lithuania for permission to move their tanks."

"I think we need to be prepared to give the Russians more than that they have to ask for permission each time," Valenti suggests.

"The Putin doctrine is saying, 'We're going to annex a chunk of Lithuania,'" Knoop says.

"If we invoke Article V, what's next?" Carr asks.

"It says an attack on one is an attack on all," Wheatley answers. "It doesn't mean we have to use force."

"Does anyone know if a country has to get access through another country?" Ellerbee, the UN ambassador, asks.

"Austria has a railway that runs through Germany," Vice President Silver says.

"Let's construct a highway that can sustain troops — a big-ass highway — and tell the Russians, 'You can't get off the highway,'" Valenti says. "You need to create the space where you can have these arguments without people losing their lives. That's what the highway does. There are historical examples."

He names a few precedents: landlocked Bolivia, which has a sovereign rail line that passes through Chile, from La Paz to Arica, and, when Slovenia was a Yugoslavian state, a road between Podsabotin and Solkan flanked by concrete walls that passed through Italy to allow Slovenians passage without having to stop at customs. Most relevant to the current crisis is the Varska-Ulitina road, which links the Baltic villages of Ulitina, Lutepaa and Sesniki, by passing through Russia. The stretch in Russian territory is lined with barbed-wire fences and guard towers, and patrolled by Russian border guards In this pressure cooker, no one remembers what's perhaps the most obvious example: the land corridors across East Germany to Berlin during the Cold War.

Wheatley's thoughts will have to wait. Before she announces a course of action, President Putin, played by Friedman, calls for a press conference in the briefing room.

Strutting to the podium wearing a black leather motorcycle jacket, he gives a spellbinding, and fear-inducing, performance.

"Has the Cold War been renewed?" one questioner asks him.

"Cold War is for those who are afraid," he says in heavily accented English.

Asked about the incursion into Lithuania, he says, "We believe the US government, like the US government in the past, will complain but will do nothing. This is part of the Russian territory. It has been part of Russian territory since Ivan the Terrible took it from Sweden in the seventeenth century. Go back and learn your history."

"Are you ready for full-blown war with the United States?" a blogger presses him. "You are aware of Article V, right?

"The Russian government is always prepared," Putin answers, blunting any doubt about his intentions.

"What is your vision of Russia in the year 2030?" an administration official asks.

"My vision is to be the most powerful country in the world," Putin says. "We are rising from the ashes of where we were fifteen years ago."

Back in the Situation Room, Montay, the secretary of defense, turns to his colleagues. "Does that make Putin's intent clear?" he asks.

"We're going to talk to France and the UK to get their help and materiel into the region and have their carrier move into the Baltic Sea," Valenti says. "We're going to reinvigorate domestic institutions such as the police. Third is to go to

Lithuania and Russia behind closed doors to say, 'We're willing to work with you to get access to Kaliningrad.' Putin can sell this however he wants."

The UN ambassador agrees. "We're not going to go to war with Russia. It's not going to happen. It's a bad idea."

As President Wheatley heads into the press briefing room where only a week earlier she'd delivered her stronger together doctrine, none of her advisers knows exactly what she'll say. "There have been some concerning events in Eurasia," she begins, standing at the lectern without notes. "We are implementing a three-pronged approach to Russia at this time. The first does involve a show of force. Congress did declare war. NATO Article V says an attack on one is an attack on all. But it is not explicitly stated there that we have to declare war. I will respect this by exploring all options. We will be meeting as the first part of our plan with NATO allies. Lithuania is a sovereign state with a right to self-defense."

She continues. "The second step is going beyond NATO." Borrowing an example from Valenti, she cites the Varska-Ulitina Road. "It is in Estonia, but it is owned by Russia. It's possible to have a strip of land pass through another country. There are about thirty of them. We will be calling for a meeting between Russia and Lithuania so that Russia can get the passage it desires. This brings space to Russia and Lithuania; the space they need.

"The third part is shoring up domestic institutions in Lithuania. Ultimately the greatest threats are to their institutions.

"We are confident of this three-pronged plan to get

through this crisis, [which is] ultimately not a crisis but a step toward becoming stronger together."

The room breaks out in applause. As it subsides, Gaddis, standing off to one side in the front of the classroom, says, "I would respectfully propose that we call an end to the simulation. It's always customary that I let Professor Hill start off."

Hill, who's beside Gaddis, clears his throat. "I thought this was excellent," he says. "The best one I've seen in many years. I think you're poised, deft, and quick . . . You had good coverage of the range of problems and a good feel for what to leave alone. You had a sense of timing. I'm in the back of the control room, but from that distance it seemed you had a timing sense that you could keep watch on a problem and see if it grew. If it grew you'd come out and meet it, and if it didn't you'd leave it alone . . . The response to the Putin doctrine was just what Putin was looking for. He's been looking for a way to break NATO. You didn't act. Our current tone is whenever there's a crisis, find a way to duck it; kick it down the road, but don't do anything with it," Hill said, reprising his frequent argument that the Obama administration has a grand strategy, and that it's one of appeasement. "We put it to you that you had to do something, and you didn't do anything." Hill later emailed a glowing assessment of Wheatley's performance. "Between the leader and the issue — that consultation with themselves — that's the grand strategic arena," he wrote. "Almost instantaneously she came up with two or three ways to deal with [the crisis], so she was acting grand strategically, although I don't think she knew it. That's a way to define grand strategy."

At the crisis simulation it is now Gaddis's turn. "I would

second with regard to overall performance. This was on the whole a very professional job. It showed a great steadiness, a great evenness . . . All of this then Madame President testifies to your skills as a leader. Whatever you did worked well, and you're to be commended. I disagreed with Professor Hill as to the outcome on the final crisis. Congress did declare an act of war. You should have signed it, but on the other hand, it was wise to note that war need not be the final option and that there can be steps that can be taken even with war declared. In a nuclear environment there have to be different understandings of declarations of war than in the past, so experimenting with different options even as war is assembled [is wise]. Your approach follows Sun Tzu's [precept] of leaving the lines of defense open. The example of the corridors was ingenious. The combination of the threat of force — the galvanizing effect of NATO would seem to create a set of pressures on President Putin other than saying the world is now going to blow up. I was particularly impressed with how you came up with these options. That's a good combination of planning for routine contingencies and fast response to things that can't be planned. Charlie and I may differ as to where this may come out, but we both admire the planning process."

Hill says: "We didn't know where we were going to go with this. We came in with eleven, twelve, thirteen [possibilities], but something happens that begins to tell us this is the one you better pay attention to. The crisis begins to speak to us, which seems to have something to do with the real world. I've seen a very few people in Washington who can do that. Something here is going on, and in a large way that's what we're hoping to get in your heads is that sense. In three out of five years we have come pretty close to predicting crises that would actually happen in the following year. We came very close to predicting Ukraine about three months before Putin took over Crimea. So watch out for what happens in the Balkans."

After the professors finish their assessments, the GSers line up for their pins, a columnar design that represents the Athenians and Spartans and the melding of different perspectives. "The idea," Hill says, "is that you wear the pin, and when you grow old you will still be able to recognize each other."

Gaddis has been standing by looking proud, and sad. "Thank all of you for participating with us. You're always welcome to participate. And you are encouraged to continue the tradition of building a GS network of alumni that extends all over the world with whom you now have a common bond. Our students five years out, ten years out are finding it nostalgic to get together and reminisce, but more than that they spend their time talking about Thucydides and Clausewitz and Machiavelli. We hope there is something that sticks with you, and we hope you will find ways to reap its rewards in ways that you cannot anticipate now."[20]

It is the last moment of the last day, and still, Gaddis is trying to prepare students for an unforeseen future.

Afterword

Since taking the long view is at the heart of grand strategy, Brady, Johnson, Chauncey, and the professors periodically discussed who could one day take over the program when Gaddis, Kennedy, and Hill decided to retire. In his memoir, Brady acknowledges at some length the difficulty for anyone of figuring out a succession plan. Advising a close friend who was unable to relinquish leadership of his firm, he told him, "If you set up a structure now, where you can coach everybody, you'll have done a real service to your legacy and to the people who are going to follow. If you don't figure it out, someone else will."[1]

In 2014 the time seemed right to address the question of GS's succession outright. By then, there was an obvious answer for the founders and donors. Not only did Elizabeth Bradley know more about GS than any faculty member outside the original program but also she was highly respected. In January 2016 she became the new director of the Brady-Johnson Program, taking over from Gaddis, who, like Kennedy and Hill, will remain a Brady-Johnson Distinguished Fellow in Grand Strategy and will teach the course into the foreseeable future.

In concert with Bradley's appointment, Yale president Salovey accepted the gift of a new chair, the Brady-Johnson Professorship in Grand Strategy, which she now occupies.

"As the grand strategy concept has picked up force as a way of thinking and teaching," Brady said on the phone, "the professorship is a daily reminder that useful human endeavors are aided by people who think across disciplines. This is the first time there's been a professorship honoring a way of teaching. It formalizes a broad way of thinking, and gives it stature within the university."[2]

Bringing a public health scholar into an area that has long belonged to history scholars and international relations practitioners highlights grand strategy's wide-ranging applicability. "What I like about Betsy being the first holder of this chair, in addition to honoring one of Yale's great scholars, teachers, and citizens," Salovey said, "is that it also reaffirms the fact that the approach of grand strategy can transcend the kinds of domains that we traditionally associate with the program."[3]

One difference between Bradley and the founding professors is her decision to state a definition of grand strategy (which she admits is only a starting place for discussion and debate): "the study of the achievement of large ends with limited means." She said, "There are many large ends in the world that we want to achieve, including peace and security, economic advancement and progress, human health, a sustainable climate, and political accountability or human rights."[4] Her background and broad view may expand the program's appeal to students who couldn't see themselves participating in grand strategy before because of its reputation for being what one alumnus described as "elite, conservative, old Yale."[5]

The ascension of a woman to the directorship will

no doubt make a difference for some students, who have complained in the past that the program lacks diversity. As a female graduate commented: "Given that the class is supposed to inspire us to see ourselves in positions of leadership and teach us what to do when we get there, I found it frustrating that I could not identify with anyone teaching the class or writing the things we read."[6]

Bradley considers her first year as a time of learning, with the change in leadership representing "evolution, not revolution." In preparation for her new post, she said, "We worked on retaining the grounding in the reading of history and classics while modernizing some of the topics and pedagogical approaches based on new realities of globalization, as well as new challenges (for example, ISIL, Ebola, and climate change) that form the context of today's students."[7]

She also engaged a new, younger set of faculty, including those from not only history but also political philosophy, organizational psychology, biology, and other disciplines. Bradley and her colleagues would emphasize the "practice of working with others toward shared objectives and the role of leadership in the process of bringing different views to bear on pressing, global problems," she said. As part of the effort to develop the program further, Bradley formed a study group with several outstanding scholars and educators at Yale including Beverly Gage, professor of history; Bryan Garsten, professor of political science and humanities and chair of the Humanities Program; David Berg, an organizational psychologist who teaches leadership and organizational effectiveness; and Kristina Talbert-Slagle, a molecular biologist who studies complex systems in cellular and human contexts. "We are living what we teach," Bradley said, "and so must use principles of grand strategy to further develop the seminar in Grand Strategy—everything is connected to everything else."[8]

Bradley continued: "How do you lead when you have a common problem—a problem where if everyone doesn't collaborate you end up doing worse? That is moving from . . . an agreed-upon Cold War approach: us or them; the US or Russia, to what is a contemporary view of being globalized: it's Russia *and* us . . . That has been in the back of Grand Strategy always . . . and may reemerge to fit the context of our future as our global resources become more constrained and as we recognize again how connected we are. Kissinger recognized the United States' interdependence in the early 1970s. But now that butterfly wing flapping halfway around the globe affects us more so than ever before. And the interconnections are endlessly unpredictable.[9]

"The challenge is to define what is Grand Strategy in that world?"[10]

Bibliography

Baker, Peter. "An Ex-President, Brush in Hand, Captures His Fellow Leaders," *New York Times,* April 4, 2014.

Berkowitz, Peter. "Our Elite Schools Have Abandoned Military History." *Wall Street Journal,* April 30, 2011, http://www.wsj.com/articles/SB10001424052748703916004576271431627026802.

Berlin, Isaiah. *The Hedgehog and the Fox: An Essay on Tolstoy's View of History.* London: Weidenfeld & Nicolson, 1953.

Bloom, Allan. *The Closing of the American Mind.* New York: Simon & Schuster, 1987.

Boorman, Scott A. *The Protracted Game: A Wei-ch'i Interpretation of Maoist Revolutionary Strategy.* Oxford: Oxford University Press,1969.

Brady, Nicholas F. *A Way of Going.* Privately printed, 2007.

Brooks, David. "Florence and the Drones." *New York Times,* February 7, 2013, http://www.nytimes.com/2013/02/08/opinion/brooks-florence-and-the-drones.html?_r=1.

Buckley, William F. Jr. *God and Man at Yale.* Washington, DC: Regnery Publishing, 1951.

Churchill, Winston. *Painting as a Pastime.* New York: Cornerstone Library Publications, 1950 (originally published in 1932 in Churchill, *Amid These Storms*).

Clausewitz, Carl von. *On War.* Edited and translated by Michael Howard and Peter Paret. Princeton: Princeton University Press, 1976.

Denby, David. *Great Books: My Adventures With Homer, Rousseau, Woolf and Other Indestructible Writers of the Western World.* New York: Simon & Schuster, 1996.

Deresiewicz, William. "Don't Send Your Kid to the Ivy League: The Nation's Top Colleges Are Turning Our Kids Into Zombies." *New Republic,* July 21, 2014.

_____. *Excellent Sheep: The Miseducation of the American Elite & the Way to a Meaningful Life.* New York: Free Press, 2014.

Doctoroff, Ariel. "Our Culture of Obsession: The Rock Stars of Yale." *Yale Herald,* October 1, 2010.

Earle, Edward Mead with Gordon A. Craig and Felix Gilbert, editors. *Makers of Modern Strategy: Military Thought from Machiavelli to Hitler.* Princeton: Princeton University Press, 1971 (originally published in 1943).

Everitt, Anthony. *Augustus: The Life of Rome's First Emperor.* New York: Random House, 2006. New York: Times Books and Henry Holt, 2010.

Farrar, Cynthia and John Lewis Gaddis. "Reflection." *Yale Daily News,* September 1, 2002.

Fitzgerald, F. Scott. "The Crack-Up." Originally published as a three-part series in the February, March, and April issues of *Esquire,* 1936, http://www.esquire.com/news-politics/a4310/the-crack-up.

Freedman, Lawrence. *Strategy: A History.* New York: Oxford University Press, 2013.

Frum, David. "Power, Terror, Peace, and War: 2.5 Cheers for George Bush." *New York Times Book Review*, June 13, 2004.

Gaddis, John Lewis. *George F. Kennan: An American Life*. New York: Penguin Press, 2011.

_____. "What Is Grand Strategy?" Keynote address, prepared as the Karl Von Der Heyden Distinguished Lecture, Duke University, February 26, 2009, for a conference on "American Grand Strategy after War," sponsored by the Triangle Institute for Security Studies and the Duke University Program in American Grand Strategy.

_____. *Surprise, Security, and the American Experience*. Cambridge, MA: Harvard University Press, 2004.

Grafton, Anthony and James Grossman. "Habits of Mind: Why College Students Who Do Serious Historical Research Become Independent, Analytical Thinkers." *American Scholar*, Winter 2015.

Griswold, Alfred Whitney. *Essays on Education*. New Haven: Yale University Press, 1954.

Hacker, Andrew and Claudia Dreifus. *Higher Education: How Colleges Are Wasting Our Money and Failing Our Kids — and What We Can Do About It*. New York: Times Books, 2010.

Hall-Palerm, Victoria. "Poise Under Pressure." *Yale Daily News*, November 14, 2014, http://yaledailynews.com/blog/2014/11/14/poise-under-pressure.

Gould, Sophie. "McCain Talks Grand Strategy." *Yale Daily News*, October 2, 2012, http://yaledailynews.com/blog/2012/10/02/mccain-talks-grand-strategy.

Hill, Charles. *Grand Strategies: Literature, Statecraft, and World Order.* New Haven: Yale University Press, 2010.

Howell, Christopher R. "From Scale to Coordination: An Intellectual History of Grand Strategy from 1815 to 1930." Yale senior thesis, May 2014.

Karabel, Jerome. *The Chosen: The Hidden History of Admission and Exclusion at Harvard, Yale, and Princeton.* New York: Mariner Books, 2006.

Keats, John. Letter to his brothers, George and Thomas. December 21, 1817, http://www.poetryfoundation.org/learning/essay/237836?page=2.

Kelley, Brooks Mather. *Yale: A History.* New Haven: Yale University Press, 1974.

Kennedy, Paul, ed. *Grand Strategies in War and Peace.* New Haven: Yale University Press, 1991.

Daniel Khalessi. "The Wall of Alexander: The Quest for a Grand Strategy in the Footsteps of Alexander and Bucephalus." April 2015, http://www.classicsofstrategy.com.

Lacy, Tim. "Establishing a Great Books Curriculum: A Brief History of the Great Books Idea." November 2005, http://www.nationalgreatbooks.com/cirriculum/background.asp.

Lalwani, Nikita and Baobao Zhang. "Married . . . with Tenure." *Yale Daily News,* April 26, 2010.

Lehmann, Nicholas. *The Big Test: The Secret History of the American Meritocracy.* New York: Farrar, Strauss, and Giroux, 1999.

Levin, Richard C. *The Work of the University.* New Haven: Yale University Press, 2003.

Machiavelli, Niccolo. *The Prince.* Translated by Harvey C. Mansfield. Chicago: University of Chicago Press, 1998.

Marcus, Amy Dockser. "Where Policy Makers Are Born." *Wall Street Journal,* December 20, 2008. http://www.wsj.com/articles/SB122973925559323583.

Mattingly, Garrett. *The Armada.* Boston: Houghton Mifflin, 1959.

Menand, Louis. *The Marketplace of Ideas: Reform and Resistance in the American University.* New York: W. W. Norton & Company, 2010.

Monty Python's Life of Brian. Warner Bros./Orion, 1979.

Obama, Barack. "Statement of the President." White House, August 28, 2014.

Pinker, Steven. "The Trouble With Harvard." *New Republic,* September 4, 2014

Sun Tzu. *The Art of War.* Translated by Samuel B. Griffith. New York: Oxford University Press, 1963.

Suri, Jeremi. *Henry Kissinger and the American Century.* Cambridge, MA: Belknap Press, 2007.

Talbott, Strobe. *The Russia Hand: A Memoir of Presidential Diplomacy.* New York: Random House, 2003.

Taylor, Mark C. *Crisis on Campus: A Bold Plan for Reforming Our Colleges and Universities.* New York: Alfred A. Knopf, 2010.

Thucydides. *The History of the Peloponnesian War.* Translated by Rex Warner, edited by M. I. Finley. Baltimore: Penguin Classics, 1954.

Walker-Wells, Evan. "Grand Strategy Spreads Across US." *Yale Herald,* March 3, 2011.

New York Times. "The War Against America; An Unfathomable Attack." September 12, 2001. http://www.nytimes.com/2001/09/12/opinion/the-war-against-america-an-unfathomable-attack.html.

Worthen, Molly. *The Man on Whom Nothing Was Lost: The Grand Strategy of Charles Hill.* New York: Houghton Mifflin, 2005.

Yale Daily News. "Heeding the Call of Our Time." September 17, 2001.

Yale Herald. "How to Get Into (and Not Get Into) That Exclusive Seminar." September 11, 2009.

Yale News. "Historic $250 Million Gift to Yale from Alumnus Is Largest Ever." September 29, 2013.

Notes

Filling a Void

1. Grand Strategy crisis simulation, December 6, 2014.

2. Patrick Leigh Fermor's books recount his walk, filled with detours and digressions, across Europe, alone at the age of eighteen, in the early 1930s.

3. "The Brady-Johnson Program in Grand Strategy at Yale University Sixth Annual Report," (2012–13), 15.

4. David Brooks, Grand Strategy dinner, Q Club, New Haven, Connecticut, October 24, 2011.

5. "Historic $250 Million Gift to Yale from Alumnus Is Largest Ever," *Yale News*, September 29, 2013.

6. Interview with Nicholas Brady, Washington, DC, 2005.

7. Nicholas F. Brady, monograph on common sense, 2005.

8. Phone interview with Charles Johnson, January 13, 2015.

9. Interview with Henry Kissinger, New York, New York, January 3, 2012.

10. Henry A. Kissinger, *White House Years* (Boston: Little, Brown, 1979), 54. I first saw this quotation in the frontispiece to Jeremi Suri's biography, *Henry Kissinger and the American Century* (Cambridge, MA: Belknap Press of Harvard University Press, 2007).

11. Interview with Charles Hill, New Haven, Connecticut, November 29, 2011.

12. William Deresiewicz, "Don't Send Your Kid to the Ivy League: The Nation's Top Colleges Are Turning Our Kids Into Zombies," *New Republic*, July 21, 2014.

13. Andrew Hacker and Claudia Dreifus, *Higher Education: How Colleges Are Wasting Our Money and Failing Our Kids — and What We Can Do About It* (New York: Times Books, 2010), 6.

14. Online Staff, "How to Get Into (and Not Get Into) That Exclusive Seminar," *Yale Herald*, September 11, 2009.

15. Interview with John Gaddis, New Haven, Connecticut, July 26, 2011.

16. Ariel Doctoroff, "Our Culture of Obsession: The Rock Stars of Yale," *Yale Herald,* October 1, 2010.

17. Gaddis interview, May 2, 2011

18. John Gaddis lecture, Yale Strategic Thinking and Foreign Affairs Symposium, New Haven, Connecticut, November 4, 2014.

19. Grand Strategy alumni survey, February 2015.

20. Ibid.

21. Interview with Richard Levin, New Haven, Connecticut, May 1, 2012.

22. Interview with Peter Salovey, New Haven, Connecticut, July 16, 2015.

23. Phone interview with Betsy Bradley, February 19, 2015; Bradley email, June 7, 2015.

Connecting to Authority

1. GS alumni survey.

2. Ibid.

3. Ibid.

4. GS class, April 16, 2012.

5. GS alumni survey.

6. Molly Worthen, *The Man on Whom Nothing Was Lost: The Grand Strategy of Charles Hill* (New York: Houghton Mifflin, 2006).

7. Gaddis, Kennedy, and Hill are also sometimes referred to as the Gang of Three, an adaptation of the Chinese Gang of Four, a political faction purged by Mao Zedong shortly before his death.

8. Deresiewicz, "Don't Send Your Kid to the Ivy League."

9. Ibid.

10. Steven Pinker, "The Trouble With Harvard," *New Republic,* September 4, 2014.

11. GS alumni survey.

12. Interview with Ewan MacDougall, Washington, DC, September 10, 2014.

13. Interview with April Lawson, Washington, DC, February 4, 2015.

14. Hill interview, May 26, 2015.

15. GS alumni survey.

16. Confidential interview, January 26, 2012.

17. Confidential phone interview, December 27, 2011.

Expanding the Community

1. GS orientation, December 5, 2011.

2. David Frum, "Power, Terror, Peace, and War: 2.5 Cheers for George Bush," *New York Times Book Review*, June 13, 2004.

3. Interview with David Brooks, Washington, DC, February 4, 2015.

4. Ibid.

Recruiting Students

1. Hill email, September 16, 2014.

2. Jeremy Friedman email, November 8, 2014.

3. GS alumni survey.

4. Deresiewicz, *Excellent Sheep: The Miseducation of the American Elite and the Way to a Meaningful Life* (New York: Free Press, 2014), 18.

5. Ibid., 16.

6. Interview with John Negroponte, New Haven to Washington, DC, Amtrak, April 18, 2011.

7. GS introductory briefing, Harkness Hall, October 8, 2014.

8. Worthen, *The Man on Whom Nothing Was Lost*, 9.

9. Interview with Ben Daus-Haberle, New Haven, Connecticut, December 12, 2011.

10. Hill email, September 14, 2014.

11. GS alumni survey.

12. Ibid.

13. Ibid.

14. Friedman email, August 27, 2015

15. GS Alumni Survey

16. Laura Wheatley is a pseudonym. Interview, New Haven, Connecticut, January 26, 2015.

17. Daus-Haberle interview, December 12, 2011.

18. GS alumni survey.

19. Ibid.

20. Ibid.

21. Wittenstein is now a lecturer at the Jackson Institute for Global Affairs and executive director of Yale's Johnson Center for the Study of American Diplomacy. Schouten is part of the Economics Sanctions and National Security division at Davis Polk.

22. GS alumni survey.

23. Ibid.

24. Ibid.

25. Ibid.

26. Ibid.

27. Interview with Norma Thompson, New Haven, Connecticut, October 17, 2011.

28. Interview with Randall Wong, New Haven, Connecticut, April 25, 2011.

29. Confidential interview, New Haven, Connecticut, October 7, 2014.

Training Hawks

1. Gaddis conversation, Spring 2011.

2. Mark Taylor, "End of the University as We Know It," *New York Times*, April 26, 2009.

3. Gaddis interview, May 2, 2011.

4. Allan Bloom, *The Closing of the American Mind* (New York: Simon & Schuster, 1987), 338–39.

5. Hill interview, March 21, 2011.

6. Ibid., August 29, 2014.

7. GS class, August 29, 2014.

8. Paul Kennedy, ed.,"Chapter One: Grand Strategies in War and Peace: Toward a Broader Definition," *Grand Strategies in War and Peace* (New Haven: Yale University Press, 1991), 5.

9. Hill interview, November 29, 2011.

10. John Gaddis, Yale symposium.

11. John Gaddis, "What Is Grand Strategy?" Prepared as the Karl Von Der Heyden Distinguished Lecture, Duke University, February 26, 2009, the keynote address for a conference on "American Grand Strategy after War," sponsored by the Triangle Institute for Security Studies and the Duke University Program in American Grand Strategy.

12. Gaddis, Yale symposium.

13. Hill interview, November 29, 2011.

14. Ibid., May 26, 2015.

15. Ibid., November 29, 2011.

16. Hill email to Gaddis, October 28, 2014.

17. Hill interview, August 29, 2014.

18. GS alumni survey.

19. Ibid.

20. Ibid.

21. Ibid. and confidential email from alumnus, March 10, 2015.

22. GS alumni survey.

23. Gaddis, Yale symposium.

24. Ibid.

25. Wong interview, April 25, 2011.

26. F. Scott Fitzgerald, "The Crack-Up," originally published as a three-part series in the February, March, and April issues of *Esquire*, 1936, http://www.esquire.com/news-politics/a4310/the-crack-up.

27. Brooks interview, February 4, 2015.

28. John Keats's letter to his brothers, George and Thomas, December 21, 1817, http://www.poetryfoundation.org/learning/essay/237836?page=2.

29. Interview with Paul Kennedy, New Haven, Connecticut, April 18, 2011.

30. The saying, originated by ancient Greek poet Archilochus, "The fox knows many things, but the hedgehog knows one big thing," was expanded upon by Oxford philosopher Isaiah Berlin in *The Hedgehog and the Fox: An Essay on Tolstoy's View of History* (London: Weidenfeld & Nicolson, 1953).

31. GS class, September 19, 2011.

32. Ibid.

33. Gaddis email, May 18, 2015.

34. Brooks interview, February 4, 2015.

Three Views on One Problem

1. John Gaddis, private journal, March 1, 1998.

2. Gaddis interview, May 2, 2011.

3. Strobe Talbott, *The Russia Hand: A Memoir of Presidential Diplomacy* (New York: Random House, 2002), 133.

4. Gaddis journal, March 1, 1998.

5. Hill interview, March 21, 2011.

6. Yale makes an effort to help its professors' spouses find jobs, whether inside or outside the university, according to an article by Nikita Lalwani and Baobao Zhang (GS '12), "Married . . . with Tenure," *Yale Daily News*, April 26, 2010; Hill interview, November 29, 2011.

7. Kennedy interview, April 11, 2011.

8. Kennedy phone interview, June 10, 2015.

9. Hill interview, May 26, 2015.

10. Ibid., March 21, 2011.

11. Ibid., November 29, 2011.

12. Kennedy phone interview, June 10, 2015.

13. Hill interview, September 19, 2013.

14. Lawrence Freedman, *Strategy: A History* (New York: Oxford University Press, 2013), 3–10.

15. Gaddis email, May 24, 2015.

16. Christopher R. Howell, "From Scale to Coordination: An Intellectual History of Grand Strategy from 1815 to 1930," May 2014 (Howell's senior thesis in humanities written under John Gaddis), 5–6. Howell draws from James L. Morrison, *The Best School in the World: West Point, the Pre-Civil War Years, 1833–1866* (Kent, OH: Kent State University Press, 1986), 47–49; and Matthew Moten, *The Delafield Commission and the American Military Profession* (College Station: Texas A & M University Press, 2000), 57.

17. Ibid., 12, 14–15.

18. Hill interview, March 21, 2011.

19. Kennedy phone interview, June 10, 2015.

20. Peter Berkowitz, "Our Elite Schools Have Abandoned Military History," *Wall Street Journal*, April 30, 2011, http://www.wsj.com/articles/SB10001424052748703916004576271431627026802.

21. Gaddis interview, May 2, 2011.

22. Louis Menand, *The Marketplace of Ideas: Reform and Resistance in the American University* (New York: W. W. Norton & Company, 2010), 54, 66–75. Menand footnotes Joan Gilbert, "The Liberal Arts College: Is It Really an Endangered Species?" *Change* 27 (September–October 1995), 36–43.

23. Kennedy interview, April 11, 2011.

24. Bernard Brodie, http://ethos.bl.uk/OrderDetails.do?uin=uk. bl.ethos.536935. William T. R. Fox, *The Super-Powers: The United States, Britain, and the Soviet Union — Their Responsibility for Peace*, (New York: Harcourt, Brace and Company, 1944).

25. Jerome Karabel, *The Chosen: The Hidden History of Admission and Exclusion at Harvard, Yale, and Princeton* (New York: Houghton Mifflin, 2005), 223.

26. Suri, 94.

27. Gaddis interview, May 2, 2011.

28. Tim Lacy, "Establishing a Great Books Curriculum: A Brief History of the Great Books Idea," November 2005, http://www.national-greatbooks.com/cirriculum/background.asp. Lacy quotes from Matthew Arnold's *Culture and Anarchy*.

29. Grand Strategy alumni survey. David Weil (GS '06), who took GS as an undergrad, said: "The readings were excellent, and as hard as Yale classes generally were, I could do all the readings; such was not the case in GS, and having to triage but be able to discuss all of them was an important skill — transferable to my time as a legislative ass't in Washington." Another GS '06 student said: "I admit I have not spent enough time with the readings. Now I regret it and am considering going back to them."

30. Menand, p. 34–35.

31. Lacy.

32. John Gaddis, reading of *George F. Kennan: An American Life* at Politics & Prose Bookstore, Washington, DC, December 8, 2011. Original reference to Edward Meade Earle, *Makers of Modern Strategy: Military Thought from Machiavelli to Hitler* (Princeton: Princeton University Press, 1943).

33. Gaddis, Politics & Prose Bookstore.

34. GS class on Thucydides, January 13, 2012.

35. Gaddis, Duke keynote address.

36. Gaddis interview, May 2, 2011.

37. GS class on Thucydides, January 13, 2012.

38. Thomas L. Friedman's "Golden Arches Theory of Conflict Prevention," from *The Lexus and the Olive Tree*, observes: "No two countries that both had McDonald's had fought a war against each other since each got its McDonald's."

39. "What we may be witnessing is not just the end of the Cold War, or the passing of a particular period of post-war history, but the end of history as such: that is, the end point of mankind's ideological evolution and the universalization of Western liberal democracy as the final form of human government." Francis Fukuyama, "The End of History?" *National Interest* (Summer 1989). Fukuyama also published a book by the same name in 1992.

40. Gaddis interview, July 27, 2011.

41. Worthen, 125.

42. Ibid.

43. Anthony Grafton and James Grossman, "Habits of Mind: Why College Students Who Do Serious Historical Research Become Independent, Analytical Thinkers," *American Scholar,* Winter 2015, 31.

44. Hill interview, March 21, 2011.

Eminent Responses

1. Gaddis memo, "Grand Strategy: Framework for a Curriculum," March 1998.

2. Gaddis journal, July 20, 1998.

3. Ibid.

4. Gaddis, Duke keynote address.

5. Gaddis email May 24, 2015.

6. Gaddis journal, November 13, 1998.

7. Gaddis, Duke keynote address.

8. Caroline Lombardo, "Summary/Assessment," Grand Strategy Conference, The Boulders, November 13–15, 1998.

9. Gaddis journal, November 14, 1998.

10. Boulders conference transcript, November 15, 1998.

11. Ibid.

12. Kennedy interview, April 11, 2011.

13. Gaddis journal, November 15, 1998.

14. Ibid.

First Year

1. Gaddis journal, February 16, 1999.

2. Ibid., June 2, 1999.

3. Interview with Caroline Lombardo, New Haven, Connecticut, January 23, 2012.

4. Gaddis journal, October 12, 1999.

5. Ibid., November 22–28, 1999.

6. Ibid., December 13, 1999.

7. Lombardo interview, January 23, 2012.

8. Hill email, May 29, 2015.

9. Ibid., September 16, 2014.

10. Deresiewicz, "Don't Send Your Kid to the Ivy League."

11. Lombardo interview, January 23, 2012.

12. Hill email, September 16, 2014.

13. Lombardo interview, January 23, 2012.

14. GS alumni survey.

15. Interview with Ted Bromund, Washington, DC, June 2011.

16. Gaddis interview, May 2, 2011.

The 9/11 Effect

1. "The War Against America; An Unfathomable Attack," *New York Times,* September 12, 2001, http://www.nytimes.com/2001/09/12/opinion/the-war-against-america-an-unfathomable-attack.html.

2. Interview with Gaddis and Cynthia Farrar, New Haven, Connecticut, March 27, 2012.

3. Ibid.

4. Farrar is also Paul Kennedy's wife.

5. Cynthia Farrar and John Lewis Gaddis, "Reflection," *Yale Daily News,* September 1, 2002.

6. Gaddis, *Surprise, Security, and the American Experience* (Cambridge, MA: Harvard University Press, 2004), 116.

7. "Heeding the Call of Our Time," *Yale Daily News,* September 17, 2001.

8. Gaddis, *Surprise,* 116.

9. Ibid., 118.

10. Confidential interview, July 2011.

11. GS alumni survey.

12. Gaddis interview, May 2, 2011.

Brady and Johnson

1. William F. Buckley Jr., *God and Man at Yale* (Washington, DC: Regnery, 1951), 12.

2. Brady, *Way of Going,* 258.

3. Phone interview with Sam Chauncey, June 2, 2015.

4. Brady, *Way of Going,* 41.

5. Conversation with Nick Brady.

6. Chauncey phone interview, June 2, 2015.

7. Levin interview, May 1, 2013.

8. Gift papers, October 2006.

9. Levin interview, May 1, 2013. The Jackson Institute was established with a gift from another distinguished Yale alumnus, John W. Jackson ('67) and his wife, Susan.

10. Gaddis interview, May 2, 2011.

11. Gaddis, Yale symposium.

Yale and Beyond

1. Malcolm Gladwell, *The Tipping Point: How Little Things Can Make a Big Difference* (Boston: Little, Brown and Co., 2000).

2. Brook Club lunch with Kennedy, Gaddis, Hill, and Brady, March 2007.

3. Interview with Elizabeth Bradley, New Haven, Connecticut, January 24, 2012.

4. Ibid.

5. Ibid.

6. Ibid.

7. Phone interview with Roger Hertog, July 1, 2015.

8. Ibid.

9. Ibid.

Making It Memorable

1. Kennedy interview, April 18, 2011.

2. GS orientation, December 5, 2011.

3. Brandon is the student's real name.

4. Toni Dorfman, associate professor of theater studies at Yale.

5. GS alumni survey.

6. Ibid.

7. Gaddis, Yale symposium.

8. Johnson phone interview, January 13, 2015.

9. Crisis simulation reporting, December 3, 2011.

Growing Cherry Trees

1. Gaddis's and Hill's writing workshop, January 9, 2012.

2. John Gaddis, "2008 Studies in Grand Strategy Writing Checklist," 1.

3. Writing workshop, January 9, 2012.

4. GS alumni survey.

5. GS orientation, December 5, 2011; GS Fifth Annual Report: 2011–12.

6. GS orientation, December 5, 2011.

7. Interview with Brandon Levin (no relation to then Yale president Richard Levin), New Haven, Connecticut, February 6, 2012.

8. Hill interview, March 21, 2011.

9. GS orientation, December 5, 2011.

10. Hill interview, November 29, 2011.

Using History

1. Freedman, *Strategy*. Isaiah Berlin, "The Hedgehog and the Fox," *The Proper Study of Mankind* (New York: Farrar, Straus and Giroux, 1997), 436–98. Winston Churchill, *Painting as a Pastime* (New York: Cornerstone Library Publications, 1950). Original publication 1932 in Churchill, *Amid These Storms*.

2. Peter Baker, "An Ex-President, Brush in Hand, Captures His Fellow Leaders," *New York Times,* April 4, 2014.

3. Brooks interview, February 4, 2015.

4. For example, in 2013 the professors substituted Anthony Everitt's biography *Augustus: The Life of Rome's First Emperor* (New York: Random House Trade Paperbacks, 2007) as the core reading for the section on the Romans for Polybius's *The Rise of the Roman Empire,* translated by Ian Scott-Kilvert (New York: Penguin Books, 1979); Plutarch's "Fabius,"

Plutarch's Lives Volume I, translated by John Drysden, edited by Arthur Hugh Clough (New York: Modern Library, 2001); selections from Livy, *The History of Rome*, translated by Aubrey de Selincourt (New York: Penguin Books, 1960); and selections from Edward Gibbon's *The History of the Decline and Fall of the Roman Empire* (New York: Penguin Classics, 1964).

5. Brooks interview, February 4, 2015.

6. GS spring syllabus, December 11, 2014, version.

7. Gaddis email, May 18, 2015.

8. Hill, *Grand Strategies*, 4.

9. GS spring syllabus, December 11, 2014, version.

10. Gaddis, Duke keynote address. Originally published in *The Landmark Thucydides: A Comprehensive Guide to The Peloponnesian War*, Richard Crawley translation, edited by Robert B. Strasser (New York: Touchstone, 1996), 16.

11. Gaddis, Duke keynote address.

12. Interview with Paul Solman, New Haven, Connecticut, September 29, 2014.

13. GS alumni survey.

14. Ibid.

15. MacDougall interview, September 10, 2014.

16. GS alumni survey.

17. Ibid.

18. Ibid.

Act One: Spring Classics

1. Sun Tzu. *The Art of War*, translated by Samuel B. Griffith (New York: Oxford University Press, 1963), 78.

2. GS class on Sun Tzu, January 9, 2012.

3. The 1939 and 1969 movies were adapted from the novella by the same name. James Hilton, *Goodbye, Mr. Chips* (Boston: Little, Brown and Company, 1934).

4. Gaddis interview, May 2, 2011.

5. GS class on Augustus, January 26, 2015.

6. Gaddis email, May 18, 2015.

7. Solman interview, September 29, 2014.

8. Gaddis interview, May 2, 2011.

9. GS orientation, December 5, 2011.

10. Confidential interview, January 13, 2012.

11. Brooks interview, February 4, 2015.

12. GS class on Thucydides, January 13, 2012.

13. Worthen, 3, 9.

14. GS class on Machiavelli, January 23, 2012.

15. Solman interview, September 29, 2014.

16. Niccolo Machiavelli, *The Prince*, translated by Harvey C. Mansfield (Chicago: University of Chicago Press, 1998), 29–30.

17. GS class on totalitarianism, April 14, 2011. http://www.epicure. demon.co.uk/whattheromans.html.

18. GS class on the Romans, January 30, 2012.

19. *Monty Python's Life of Brian*, WB/Orion, 1979.

20. GS class on totalitarianism, April 4, 2012.

21. GS class on Sun Tzu, January 9, 2012.

22. Phone interview with Scott Boorman, March 31, 2015.

23. GS class on Sun Tzu, January 9, 2012.

24. Gaddis interview, May 2, 2011.

25. Negroponte interview, April 18, 2011.

26. Levin interview, May 1, 2012.

27. *The Prince*.

28. GS class on Machiavelli, January 28, 2013.

29. David Brooks, "Florence and the Drones," *New York Times*, February 7, 2013. http://www.nytimes.com/2013/02/08/opinion/brooks-florence-and-the-drones.html?_r=1&module=ArrowsNav&contentCollection=Opinion&action=keypress&region=FixedLeft&pgtype=article

30. Negroponte interview, April 18, 2011.

31. GS class on the Romans, January 30, 2012.

32. GS class on Thucydides, January 13, 2012.

33. GS class on Sun Tzu, January 9, 2012.

34. Negroponte email, March 28, 2016.

35. GS class on Sun Tzu, January 9, 2012.

Act Two: Summer Odyssey

1. GS alumni survey.
2. Confidential interview, December 27, 2011.
3. Gaddis, Duke keynote address. He quotes from Carl von Clausewitz, *On War*, edited and translated by Michael Howard and Peter Paret (Princeton: Princeton University Press, 1976), 113.
4. Paul Kennedy, The Nuts and Bolts of Grand Strategy workshop, January 23, 2012.
5. GS orientation, December 5, 2011.
6. Hill interview, May 26, 2015.
7. Gaddis, Duke keynote address.
8. Friedman email, August 27, 2015.
9. Deresiewicz, *Excellent Sheep*, 18.
10. Interview with Conor Crawford, New Haven, Connecticut, September 20, 2011.
11. GS alumni survey.
12. GS alumni survey; Blomerth emails, June 14 and June 22, 2015.
13. Confidential email, June 2, 2015.
14. Interview with Daniel Khalessi, New Haven, Connecticut, December 12, 2014; Daniel Khalessi, "The Wall of Alexander: The Quest for a Grand Strategy in the Footsteps of Alexander and Bucephalus," http://www.classicsofstrategy.com, April 2015.
15. Ibid.
16. GS alumni survey.
17. Ibid.
18. Gaddis, Duke keynote address.

Act Three: Fall Boot Camp

1. GS class, August 29, 2014.
2. Barack Obama, "Statement from the President," White House, August 28, 2014.
3. GS class, August 29, 2014.
4. Marshall Briefs handout.
5. Victoria Hall-Palerm, "Poise Under Pressure," *Yale Daily News*, November 14, 2014; http://yaledailynews.com/blog/2014/11/14/poise-under-pressure/.

6. Sophie Gould, "McCain Talks Grand Strategy," *Yale Daily News,* October 2, 2012; http://yaledailynews.com/blog/2012/10/02/mccain-talks-grand-strategy/.

7. GS policy brief on Africa, September 29, 2014.

8. Interview with Leo Montay (class pseudonym extended), October 27, 2014. Phone interview took place on June 25, 2015.

9. GS policy brief on Africa, September 29, 2014.

10. Interview with Justin Schuster, New Haven, Connecticut, December 12, 2014.

11. Schuster email, December 19, 2014.

12. Confidential email to Hill and Gaddis, July 1, 2015. Some of the identifying details were changed.

13. GS alumni survey.

14. Interview with Ted Bromund, New Haven, Connecticut, July 26, 2011.

15. Gaddis,Yale symposium.

16. GS class, December 1, 2014.

17. Ibid.

18. GS alumni survey.

19. Ibid.

20. Ibid.

21. Strategic Thinking in Public Health class, February 15, 2012.

22. Hill email, March 10, 2014.

23. Schuster interview, December 12, 2014.

24. Confidential phone interview, December 27. 2011.

25. Schuster interview, December 12, 2014.

26. Montay interview, October 6, 2014.

27. Confidential phone interview, December 27, 2011.

28. Lawson interview, February 4, 2015.

29. Montay phone interview, June 25, 2015.

30. GS policy brief on Africa, October 27, 2014.

31. Hill email to Gaddis, October 27, 2014.

32. Ibid., October 28, 2014.

33. GS class, December 1, 2014.

34. Hall-Palerm, "Poise Under Pressure."

35. GS class, December 1, 2014.

36. Ibid.

Act Four: Winter Leadership

1. GS class, December 1, 2014.

2. Friedman email, August 27, 2015.

3. GS class, December 1, 2014.

4. Wheatley interview, January 26, 2015.

5. GS class, December 1, 2014.

6. GS crisis simulation, December 3, 2011.

7. GS crisis simulation, December 6, 2014.

8. GS alumni survey

9. Crisis simulation, December 6, 2014.

10. Wheatley interview, January 26, 2015.

11. Kissinger, *White House Years*, p. 54.

12. Phone interview with George Shultz, February 2, 2012.

13. GS crisis simulation, Decembr 6, 2014.

14. Wheatley interview, January 26, 2015.

15. GS crisis simulation, December 6, 2014.

16. Phone interview with Laura Wheatley, December 11, 2014.

17. Strutmore Strategic Analysis.

18. Hill email, December 9, 2014.

19. GS crisis simulation, December 13, 2014.

20. Ibid

Afterword

1. Brady, *Way of Going*, 165.

2. Brady phone interview, June 2015.

3. Salovey interview, July 16, 2015.

4. Bradley interview, May 26, 2015.

5. GS alumni survey.

6. Ibid.

7. Bradley email, July 5, 2015.

8. Ibid., August 3, 2015

9. MIT meteorologist Edward Lorenz articulated the "butterfly effect"—the notion that infinitesimal events can have widespread, and unpredictable, consequences; Bradley interview, May 26, 2015.

10. Bradley interview, May 26, 2015.

Index